Formula 1

IN CAMERA 1970–79

Volume Two

Formula 1
IN CAMERA 1970–79

Paul Parker

Volume Two

First published in June 2012
Reprinted in October 2012

A catalogue record for this book is available
from the British Library

ISBN 978 0 85733 074 1

Library of Congress catalog card no. 2011946144

Haynes North America Inc.,
861 Lawrence Drive,
Newbury Park, California 91320, USA

Published by Haynes Publishing,
Sparkford, Yeovil, Somerset BA22 7JJ, UK
Tel: 01963 442030 Fax: 01963 440001
Int. tel: +44 1963 442030
Int. fax: +44 1963 440001
E-mail: sales@haynes.co.uk
Website: www.haynes.co.uk

Printed in the USA by Odcombe Press LP,
1299 Bridgestone Parkway, La Vergne, TN 37086

All photographs courtesy LAT Photographic except:

Michael Cooper Archive: 15

Grand Prix Library: 14btm, 27btm, 31top, 33btm, 39, 42top, 44btm, 73top, 74,
140btm, 150top, 154, 217, 230, 234

Klemantaski Collection: 18

Sutton Images: 7, 10, 11, 14top, 16top, 23, 25btm, 28btm, 29, 30, 36btm, 43,
44top, 49btm, 51, 52, 54btm, 59, 61top, 62, 63top, 64, 69, 70, 71btm, 73btm, 75top,
76btm, 77, 80-82, 85, 87-92, 93btm, 96btm, 97top, 98btm, 99, 100btm, 101, 104,
105, 107, 109, 110, 112, 114top, 115, 117top, 118, 119btm, 123, 125, 127-129, 133,
136, 137btm, 138, 140top, 141, 142, 144btm, 145, 150btm, 151-153, 157top, 158top,
160-162, 163btm, 168, 172, 173, 176top, 177top, 178top, 181btm, 185btm, 187,
188btm, 189, 191btm, 197-199, 202, 203top, 205, 206, 210, 211top, 213, 219, 224,
228, 229btm, 233top, 235btm

AUTHOR'S INTRODUCTION

Readers of my *Formula 1* and *Sports Car Racing in Camera* series might be familiar with the original *Formula 1 in Camera 1970–79* of some years ago that featured the work of Rainer Schlegelmilch, who is still photographing F1 today.

This was the first of the genre, but it did not cover all the grands grix during the decade as Rainer concentrated mainly on the European races, with rare exception, at the time. He did not attend any of the South African GPs in period, the US GP (West) at Long Beach in 1978, the US GPs (East) at Watkins Glen, the Canadian GPs or the Japanese GPs. Volume Two incorporates the missing races and also seeks to give more attention to the less-well-known participants, so it does not just concentrate on the more familiar faces and teams.

For those coming to this era for the first time I would respectfully suggest that the Schlegelmilch book, which features chapter intros and team entries/stats for each year, might be of interest. Whereas Volume Two has explanatory, extended captions I have tried not to replicate the content of the first volume, and these two editions complement each other. Additionally this is self-evidently a pictorial record of the era that does not claim to be a definitive record of all and sundry – to achieve this would have required 1,000 pages.

So, welcome to a decade that in its final years looks surprisingly modern, certainly not from 33 years ago. By 1979 most of the circuits were Armco lined, the cars looked very high tech, even if by modern standards they were relatively basic, whilst the drivers were all but invisible and covered from head to toe in protective clothing festooned with sponsors' logos. As noted elsewhere, media-driven commercial sponsorship quickly became necessary for professional motor sport to survive, let alone prosper.

This level of overt advertising was, until 1968/69, essentially alien to European motor sport, if not in American circles, so its impact was all the more effective and, for some, vulgar and intrusive. Of course, the full panoply of global marketing and choice were not yet possible because there was no internet, no mobile phones and networks as we know them today – no Blackberries, no iPhones or any other 'online' access.

Televised motor sport in Britain had always been treated with a certain contempt and disdain, although finally in the 1970s this began to improve. One positive aspect of this limited broadcast media coverage (in Britain) was that the race reports which graced the pages of *Autosport* and *Motor Sport*, were not only informative but enjoyable to read and often controversial. Reading back through these old journals I was struck by how outspoken and, by modern standards, politically incorrect and honest various journalists and racers were.

Some of the comments in the late Nick Brittan's 'Private Ear' column are very blunt indeed and would not be allowed today. Or how about the late Denny Hulme, in his regular 'Behind the Wheel' pieces for *Autosport*, describing Mario Andretti as 'SuperWop'. Such good-humoured name-calling today would no doubt result in accusations of racism and worse, and the writer becoming permanently persona non grata and possibly prosecuted.

Back then, however, reality was in charge and, safety aside, all the better for it.

Paul Parker
Summer 2012

▶ Jo Ramirez was a friend of Pedro and Ricardo Rodriguez, and accompanied the latter in his brief time as a Ferrari driver during 1961/62. Later on he worked for Dan Gurney with the F1 Eagles of 1966/67 and also on the team's Can-Am, TransAm and Indycar activities. Following a stint at the John Wyer/Gulf team he joined Tyrrell after which he worked for Copersucar, Shadow, ATS, Theodore and most famously McLaren, retiring in 2001. He attends Patrick Depailler's Tyrrell 005 on the scales at Interlagos before the 1974 Brazilian GP.

1970

THE WRONG FERRARI WON THE ITALIAN GP

Brabham and the new March 701 began the year in winning form, but the former unnecessarily lost two races to Jochen Rindt's Lotus and also suffered severe reliability issues later in the year. March won three F1 races (two were non-championship) but gradually lost ground despite employing Chris Amon and supplying cars to Tyrrell for Jackie Stewart. Chapman's Lotus 72 underwent numerous changes to become successful and after winning four GPs in a row retired in Austria and then crashed during Monza practice killing Rindt. His was the third F1 driver fatality of 1970, Bruce McLaren and Piers Courage having perished in June. BRM recovered thanks to the new P153 and Pedro Rodriguez whilst Matra reappeared without winning anything whilst McLaren were badly affected by their founder's death and Hulme's Indy injuries. Ferrari meanwhile had started poorly and Jacky Ickx posted five dnfs in the first seven GPs before finishing second in Germany and winning in Austria. However he retired at Monza whilst teammate Regazzoni won the race but Ickx finished first in Canada, a delayed fourth in America (won fortuitously by Lotus rookie Emerson Fittipaldi) and won the final GP in Mexico. It was not enough to overtake Rindt's modest 45-point score so the Austrian was a posthumous World Champion five points ahead of the Belgian but ultimately it came back to this, the wrong Ferrari won the Italian GP.

⬇ More understeer for monsieur? The Italian GP and Jacky Ickx in the Ferrari 312B/003 spare during Monza practice at the Parabolica. In Ferrari terms the wrong car won at Monza, if Ickx's race chassis 001 had not suffered clutch failure then the Belgian, who had started from pole and led the race, might have been the 1970 F1 World Champion. Meanwhile, teammate Clay Regazzoni had no such problems and drove to victory in front of a jubilant crowd, whose enthusiasm following Rindt's death was poorly received in some quarters. Attitudes were rather more robust in those days, and death was still a matter largely for family, friends, and colleagues rather than overt public grief.

⬉ Five of the new March 701s, launched to great acclaim at Silverstone on 6 February, attended the opening race of the 1970 F1 World Championship at Kyalami, the two works 701s of Amon and Siffert, Andretti's Granatelli car, and the two Tyrrell entries for Stewart and Servoz-Gavin. Amon was joint fastest in practice with Stewart but it was the Scot who led the race until his tyres went 'off', ultimately finishing third. Amon was hit by Rindt's works Lotus 49C and later suffered a welding failure in the coolant system, which overheated the engine. The same problem struck Andretti's 701, while Siffert's car, 701/5 seen here, finished a lacklustre tenth. The race was won by Jack Brabham in his new BT33 ahead of Hulme's McLaren and Stewart's March.

⬅ Lotus 49 R8 began life as Graham Hill's 1969 Tasman mount and was ultimately the most raced 49 of the era, with 42 starts during 1969–72. It was de facto a hybrid car, being part 49 and part 49B. Following Richard Attwood's fourth place at Monaco, R8 was upgraded and acquired by Jo Bonnier, who entered it for the 1969 British GP, but it was commandeered by Lotus after Graham Hill rejected the 4WD 63. Bonnier raced it at the Nürburgring where he retired with a fuel leak (a recurring problem with R8). Then the front suspension collapsed during practice for the Oulton Park Gold Cup, after which Bonnier gave the car back to Lotus having never paid for it. It was bought by Dave Charlton in late 1969, although actually paid for (£20,000) by construction company-owner Aldo Scribante, a sponsor of South African drivers at the time. In January 1970 it received the latest 49C updates and at Kyalami the colourful Scuderia Scribante-liveried Lotus of Charlton qualified 13th, quickest of the local drivers. In the race a probable points finish was lost when the left rear Firestone tyre threw a tread, and following a long pit stop (caused by the stuck rear wheel) the engine refused to restart.

⬆ Tony Southgate joined BRM in 1969 and designed the P153 for 1970. The new car was very low set with 13in-diameter wheels all round, and Southgate recalls in his autobiography *From Drawing Board to Chequered Flag* that it reflected his obsession with a low centre of gravity. The original Geoff Johnson two-valve V12 engine was redesigned by Aubrey Woods with a four-valve cylinder head for the P153. Two were entered at Kyalami for Pedro Rodriguez and Jackie Oliver, whilst Canadian George Eaton drove the old P139. Oliver was the quickest BRM in qualifying, but he retired, and Pedro finished ninth. Southgate had the cars repainted in a Vauxhall dark green, but it was soon to be replaced by the Yardley livery. Here Jackie, with his distinctive striped peak helmet, is caught by the camera having a 'moment'. The vertical stripes had originated years before to distinguish Oliver from Jim Clark, their dark-coloured helmets and white peaks looking similar in period black and white images.

← Two weeks after Kyalami the non-championship Race of Champions included Jean-Pierre Beltoise with one of the new Matra MS120s which had finished fourth and seventh at Kyalami. Beltoise non-started after crashing MS120/1 during practice, losing two wheels and damaging the monocoque. The Bernard Boyer-designed MS120 was the successor to the Cosworth DFV-powered MS80 that had taken Jackie Stewart to his first World Championship in 1969. Vélizy had resurrected their raucous 1968 V12 because Matra had been taken over by Chrysler's French subsidiary Simca. Redesigned with central induction trumpets it was claiming an optimistic 450bhp. The 60° four-valve V12 engine layout afforded a lower centre of gravity than its DFV-powered predecessor and it weighed 1,206lb (548kg) with fluids. Transmission was courtesy of Hewland's FG400 gearbox, and in this guise it is using 15in rear wheels with inboard rear brakes. Jean-Pierre is otherwise distracted as a member of the press (presumably) snaps away; I wonder who she was?

↑ Peter Gethin's 1969 F5000 championship-winning season in a semi-works McLaren M10A earned him a F1 seat with McLaren for 1970, and this was his inaugural drive for the team at Brands Hatch. He is driving Denny Hulme's 1969 chassis M7A/2, the Mexican GP-winning car. Gethin started from the penultimate row, but only 1.2sec slower than Hume's second-row time in the later M14, going on to finish sixth in the race. The race was won by Stewart's Tyrrell March after Brabham was delayed by a faulty coil, the Australian dropping to fourth. This was an omen of what would be a very frustrating final year in racing for the three-times F1 World Champion.

The Spanish GP welcomed Colin Chapman's replacement for the ageing Lotus 49, the Maurice Phillippe-designed 72, a radical-looking and radically different car, which made its debut at Jarama. Two were entered for Jochen Rindt and John Miles but there were problems with front brake heat insulation, wayward handling, excessive roll, and assorted other teething troubles, including overheating. The cars used 15in-diameter rear wheels and 13in fronts, and on Rindt's chassis R2 the original solid front discs were replaced with ventilated ones. These were inboard, hence the air extractor outlets behind the NASA ducts, and the car features the anti-dive, anti-squat suspension, which would be abandoned pre-Monaco. Note the three-tier rear wing. This is chassis 72/R1 that Miles failed to qualify, whilst Rindt started from the outside of the third row, which flattered the car, but it soon retired because of ignition failure. Aside from the 72s, Chapman also entered Spaniard Alex Soler-Roig in a 49C, but this too failed to make the grid.

This is the new Brabham BT33 that made its debut at Kyalami, where Jack Brabham took his final GP victory. It was Ron Tauranac's first monocoque F1 design, partly responding to regulatory changes that demanded enclosed rubber fuel cells (although he had previously designed and built the monocoque BT25 Indy car). The other works Brabham BT33 was for renowned Porsche sports car racer Rolf Stommelen with backing from Ford Germany and entered by the German motoring magazine *Auto Motor und Sport*. Stommelen's BT33/1 at Jarama reveals its slightly wider monocoque, the original being marginal on fuel capacity at the higher consumption circuits, this configuration accommodating bigger tanks. Brabham retired just as he was about to take the lead, whilst Stommelen's engine failed. The Spanish GP started with a first-lap accident when Oliver's BRM P153 suffered a front stub axle breakage and T-boned Ickx's Ferrari 312B, both cars being destroyed by fire. As a precaution, Pedro Rodriguez in the other BRM P153 was withdrawn after four laps. Jackie Stewart won the Spanish GP for Ken Tyrrell, with Bruce McLaren second, his last points-scoring finish.

⬆ Next stop was Silverstone's XXII Daily Express International Trophy for F1/F5000 cars on 26 April, a non-championship event. Chris Amon was driving a works Ferrari 512S at the Monza 1,000km and, despite flying to and fro, managed to set fastest time on the dry Friday before returning to Monza on Saturday where he finished second. It was a two-heat event and Amon won race one from Stewart by 12.1sec, and was content to follow Stewart home in race two, winning on aggregate by 10.2sec. In race one Amon, in March 701/1 with visor up, is looking across at Stewart in 701/2, with Hulme McLaren M14A/2 and Gethin in the F5000 McLaren-Chevy M10B alongside on the front row of the 4 3 4 grid. Hulme finished sixth overall and Gethin won the F5000 class in heat one but retired in heat two. It was the third consecutive and final F1 victory for the March 701 and ended the mutual dissatisfaction 'twixt team and driver for now, Mosley being concerned about the cost of employing Chris, and the driver unhappy with preparation standards. Further down the grid, Rindt's Lotus 72 finished fifth in heat one and retired in heat two; the car was still far from right.

 Following the end of his Honda tenure and a disastrous year at BRM in 1969, John Surtees was awaiting his new DFV-powered Len Terry-designed Surtees TS7 for 1970. In the interval between he purchased this ex-works McLaren M7C/1, the one and only such car based upon a F5000 chassis, which was driven by Bruce McLaren during 1969. Surtees first raced it at Kyalami, and here during a Monaco practice session he rounds the Gasworks hairpin, arms well cranked over. He ended up towards the rear of the grid and retired early in the race with low oil pressure. Note the differing road surfaces that are liberally stained with oil.

 Graham Hill finished sixth at Kyalami and fourth at Jarama, but uncharacteristically crashed Rob Walker's Lotus 49C (R7) – Jo Siffert's 1968 British GP-winning car – at Monaco. When John Miles failed to qualify the works 49C (R10) despite outpacing slowest man Pedro Rodriguez whose 'seeded' status took priority, Walker asked Colin Chapman if he could borrow R10. This was agreed and the car was repainted, but Graham had to start at the back of the grid, as he had not qualified R10. Hill rounds Tabac on his way to fifth place, and note the Lotus 72 three-tiered rear wing. R10 was originally chassis R5, Hill's 1968 Monaco winner. In 1969 it was renumbered R10 and provided Graham's fifth and final Monaco victory. So Graham had raced it at three consecutive Monaco GPs, but on a darker note it was also the car he crashed at Watkins Glen in 1969. The race itself was famously won by Jochen Rindt's works Lotus 49C/R6 from behind after a poor practice following the retirements of the Stewart and Amon March 701s. In the closing stages, leader Jack Brabham was delayed by backmarkers but was still ahead until distracted on that fateful last corner and missed his braking point. Thus Rindt won a race that he had only led for a few seconds over the last few hundred yards.

 Derek Bell became one of the best sports car racers of his era, winning five Le Mans plus the World Sportscar Championship in 1985/86. Paradoxically his F1 career that began at Ferrari in 1968 was effectively one cul de sac after another. A brief flirtation with McLaren's unsuccessful 4WD M9A in the 1969 British GP followed, and later there was more of the same. However, nil desperandum, and Derek was entered at the 1970 Belgian GP in Tom Wheatcroft's ex-works Brabham BT26A/4 (he had also attended the Brands Hatch ROC in March but non-started after crashing during practice). The Church Farm, Pagham, address on the transporter in Spa's paddock is reference to his stepfather Bernard Hender, who entered Bell in his early days and later in F2 under the name Church Farm Racing. Derek qualified the now outclassed car towards the rear of the grid and retired after one lap because of gear linkage problems. This was his last appearance in the car.

Having followed Chris Amon past Stewart at the Belgian GP, Pedro Rodriguez then took the lead in the Yardley-liveried BRM P153/02 and, except very briefly, stayed there to the end. Amon was nonplussed, the BRM not having been quick in practice, and despite all his efforts, including setting fastest lap and taking the Masta kink absolutely flat out which took him past Pedro, by Stavelot the BRM was leading again. It was BRM's first GP win since Monaco 1966 and this led to unsubstantiated accusations for decades after that the BRM had been using an oversize engine in the race. It was also Pedro's second and final GP win, and chassis 02's last race. Tony Southgate told the author in 2000 that the BRM's oil system was inadequate and at high rpm the engine required a vast amount of lubricant circulating to keep it safe (this is also why they dropped oil), which led to a 4.5-gallon oil tank. It was Dunlop's final GP victory as they withdrew from F1 at the end of the year.

Ronnie Peterson made his F1 debut at Monaco for well-known historic racer Colin Crabbe of Antique Automobiles where he finished seventh and last in March 701/8. The Swede lined up ninth-quickest at Spa, just a tenth quicker than works driver Jo Siffert. This was a very tight run ship, the team having only one engine, and their troubles began when Peterson accidentally ran over a policeman's foot whilst trying to get into the circuit pre-race. He was locked up and only released after pressure from the race organisers. Alas, the March misbehaved and Ronnie finished unclassified eight laps down. As he climbed out of the car he was rearrested and spent two days in the cells before release on promising to return to face justice, although the matter was eventually dropped. Here Peterson blasts round Spa at some huge velocity past the inadequate two-tier Armco, the March's springs compressed against the forces of gravity.

⬆ Bespectacled Andrea de Adamich and the new Alfa Romeo T33 V8-powered McLaren M14D/1 in Zandvoort's crowded pit lane, an unsuccessful combination that frequently failed to qualify. Phil Kerr in *To Finish First* (Motor Racing Publications, 2008) recalled that the Autodelta-built sports car engines varied greatly in power and were unreliable as well as late on delivery. To quote Patrick McNally's *Autosport* race report, 'George Eaton, having failed to qualify all season, looked as though he was out of luck again, until mitigation by Louis Stanley (BRM) at the end of the day was rewarded with the discovery of a lap which gave him the last available place … the Italian was understandably annoyed to be pushed off the grid by Eaton with a time that was only discovered several hours after practice.' McLaren had withdrawn from the Belgian GP following Bruce McLaren's death at Goodwood and Hulme's burnt hands from an Indy smash resulted in them fielding Dan Gurney and Peter Gethin in his first GP start here. They both retired early on, Gurney with engine failure and Gethin understeering off the road, but the M7C/1 of John Surtees finished sixth. In the background are Jochen Rindt with Lotus mechanics Graham Bartells and the partially hidden Eddie Dennis.

◄ Finally the Lotus 72 performed as it should at Zandvoort, courtesy of a new and stiffer monocoque plus conventional suspension – gone was the anti-dive, anti-squat set-up. Jochen Rindt started from pole position ahead of Stewart's March and the Ickx Ferrari, and after following the latter for two laps took the lead, finally winning by 30sec from Stewart with Ickx third. John Miles in the other 72 finished seventh but twice lapped. It was to be the first of four consecutive GP victories for a distraught Rindt devastated by the death of his close friend Piers Courage, who had died in a fiery crash in the Williams de Tomaso. It is interesting to note that from Zandvoort onwards Rindt was using the lighter FG series Hewland gearbox, once considered marginal in durability terms for the torquey DFV but now much improved by stronger gear wheels and other enhancements.

◣ For the second year in succession the French GP was run on the Charade circuit near Clermont Ferrand. It was comprised of rugged, twisting road in the hills of the Auvergne of just over 5 miles (8.055km) in length, the very antithesis of purpose-built modern F1 and media-dependent facilities. A troubled-looking Dan Gurney sits in his McLaren M14A/1 at his penultimate GP in the Charade pits during practice. He went on to finish sixth, his last point-scoring finish, and then retired in the British GP ending a F1 career that had begun with Ferrari at the Dutch GP, Zandvoort, in 1959.

► Jacky Ickx started from pole position in Ferrari 312B/003 and led the French GP from fellow front row occupant Beltoise's Matra for 14 laps by an increasing margin, followed by Stewart's March, which developed ignition problems. Stewart eventually finished ninth despite stopping for repairs and a broken rear roll bar. Ickx's Ferrari expired with valve failure on lap 17, leaving Beltoise in the lead until hindered by a deflating rear tyre, eventually pitting on lap 27 before stopping on lap 35 with fuel starvation, finally being classified 13th. Here Ickx heads Jean-Pierre in the Matra MS120/3 past a rock face, the original immovable object and just what you need at a F1 track. The demise of the V12s left Rindt to win the race ahead of Amon's March 701, a tremendous achievement against the much superior Lotus 72.

◁ So far the season had been dominated by Cosworth DFV-powered cars, with only a BRM victory at Spa intruding upon the V8 hegemony. However, some were convinced that the V12s would overwhelm Keith Duckworth's masterpiece, now in its fourth season, and Ferrari looked the most likely to achieve this. Here is Canadian supermarket heir George Ross Eaton (born 12 November 1945) whose F1 career was spent with BRM from 1969–1971. There were three BRM P153s at the British GP for Rodriguez, Oliver, and this one (chassis 03) for Eaton. They qualified fourth (Oliver), 15th (Rodriguez) and 16th (Eaton). However, all three retired at Brands Hatch, because of, respectively, engine failure, an accident, and low oil pressure. In the picture we can see the blond-haired Eaton in his cowboy boots, with Pedro Rodriguez in the background beside his P153/05. Also visible in the narrow pit lane is a Ford Cortina 1600E, a period favourite with its Rostyle wheels and 'de luxe' trim.

⬆ The first thing you notice about this picture is just how fine Jochen Rindt judged his gap, or Brabham allowed perhaps. Nowadays such moves are unremarkable, but then it was a case of get it right or anything could happen, and sometimes did. Look at the flimsy wing stays on the Lotus, and Ickx leading in his Ferrari 312B/003 with its distinctive gold wheels. Brabham retook the lead on lap 65 after the Austrian missed a gear, but ran out of fuel on the last lap when leading. Ron Dennis, then a Brabham mechanic, admitted years later that he had left the car on too rich a mixture setting, so Brabham lost another race to Rindt on the final lap. Post race scrutineering revealed that the Lotus rear wing stays were bent, and Dean Delamont of the RAC ordered chief mechanic Dick Scammell to straighten them, but he refused until he had spoken to Colin Chapman, so Delamont disqualified the car. Chapman appealed and the stays were straightened and reset, giving Rindt a pyrrhic victory. Allegedly Colin had raised the wing above the allowed height to improve the handling, and the mechanics who knew this had leant on it after the race, but too much, hence the buckled supports.

↑ In 1970 it was decided to boycott the German GP at the Nürburgring, so the race was held at the Hockenheim circuit. The decision had resulted in accusations of cowardice from various quarters, which GPDA President Joachim Bonnier responded to in a letter to *Autosport* published on 24 September 1970. In it he pointed out a meeting had been held with the organisers on 10 June 1968 discussing safety improvements for drivers and spectators, which was confirmed by Nürburgring GmbH with a verbal agreement to complete these measures over a two- to three-year period. In reality only 25–33% of the work had been completed in the intervening period when the circuit was inspected on 3 August 1970 despite claims to the contrary. Bonnier finished his letter by stating that: 'We do not particularly like to be called cowards, which I do not think we are, but we would at any time prefer that to not trying to make motor racing – the greatest of all sports – also the best of all sports, safer.' Here is Ron Dennis, who was attending Brabham's BT33 just behind, looking intently at Emerson Fittipaldi's Team Lotus 49C R10 as 'Herbie' Blash signs a form for a scrutineering official. This was Fittipaldi's second GP start for Lotus and having finished a respectable 8th at the British GP he was to be a worthy 4th at Hockenheim.

Following Zandvoort Frank Williams missed the French GP but returned at Brands Hatch with Brian Redman and a new de Tomaso chassis 505-38-3. This was withdrawn after a hub failure, and Hockenheim was to be another disappointment. In *Autosport* Patrick McNally observed that 'Brian Redman started off with the wrong ratios, then had ignition trouble, and finally, just when he was getting going, spun and put it into the sand at the second chicane.' It was Redman's final outing in the car (Tim Schenken drove it for the remainder of 1970 without success, after which the 505 went back to de Tomaso) and here Frank talks to Redman in the Dunlop-shod H.W. Ward Machine Tools-sponsored car. Later in the year Brian announced his retirement from racing and moved to Johannesburg, which turned out to be short-lived. The race became a tremendous scrap for the lead between Rindt and Ickx, bar the intrusion of Regazzoni's sister Ferrari until it retired. Eventually Ickx led with two laps to go, but following a mistake by Jochen, Ickx lifted off to avoid a collision and Rindt went on to win the race by a mere 0.7sec.

March's policy of making as many cars as possible to turn a profit almost backfired at Hockenheim. BMW-contracted Hubert Hahne was a successful touring car racer who had raced for them in F2. He purchased this new 701/9 and entered it for the German GP but failed to qualify, claiming that the car was uncompetitive. Writs were issued and as March returned from the Austrian GP via Germany their cars were temporarily impounded by the German police. However, Max Mosley persuaded Hahne to bring his car to Silverstone where Ronnie Peterson was to try to match an agreed time, and if he failed Hahne would win his case. Inevitably Ronnie proceeded to better it by 2sec, so Hahne went back to Germany and retired from racing after the Italian GP, citing Rindt's death as the reason. The March was entered at Hockenheim by Hahne but its smart silver livery bore witness to its sponsor, German publishing magnate Axel Springer (2 May 1912 – 22 September 1985).

◄ Arguably two of the greatest racing drivers of this time share the pits trackside wall with its English NO SMOKING sign at the Österreichring in the Mur valley near Zeltweg in northern Styria. In the background is a typical Alpine scene, a lake and the Seetal Alps. The first Austrian GP had been held on Zeltweg airfield in 1964, which resulted in a victory for Ferrari and Lorenzo Bandini, but it did not return to the World Championship calendar until 1970 with a new, much longer, and purpose-built circuit (described by BRM driver Jackie Oliver as very scary and unfinished), which was to be an emphatic triumph for Maranello. In the race Mario crashed out on lap 14 in his final March drive in the Andy Granatelli car, whilst Jackie only lasted eight laps because of a split fuel line.

▶ Jochen Rindt's final GP start resulted in a retirement due to a broken camshaft (it was DFV 901, the Hockenheim motor) and Rindt seemed quite relaxed about this. During practice the scrutineers had been complaining that the 72 was too wide where the side radiators were mounted, but this did not stop Rindt from taking pole position. In the race he briefly ran third behind the Ferrari duo of 'Jackson' and 'Reggae' but dropped back on oil from Cevert's exploding DFV and then ran in the second group adrift of the leading Ferraris and Beltoise's Matra before the engine failure. Lotus No. 2 John Miles's race was even shorter, lasting three laps before the left front brake-shaft broke. Years later Miles observed that he was probably over-cautious and thought too much, which is why he was not a successful F1 driver, but was still alive.

▶ The Austrian GP was Ferrari's first World Championship victory since Rouen in 1968 (Ickx) and also the last time that a 12-cylinder car had won a GP. Nevertheless, the ever-improving Regazzoni out-qualified his illustrious teammate and led the first lap, after which Ickx assumed the lead and stayed there, winning by just 0.61sec from his Swiss No. 2. The third Ferrari of Ignazio Giunti occupied fourth place until he had to pit to replace a front tyre, and finally finished seventh. It was the beginning of a Maranello renaissance that almost changed the status quo. This is Ickx's 312B/001 with its chrome-plated Sebring Mach 1 mirrors, also used by BRM and the works Marches, which were a popular accessory for road cars of this period.

Jackie Oliver and John Surtees had quite a dice in both heats of the non-championship Gold Cup at Oulton Park, and this is Oliver in the BRM P153/04 followed by an almost hidden Surtees in his TS7/001. In heat one Surtees finished first 6.6sec ahead of Oliver, and in heat two he finished second behind Rindt's Lotus 72 and 13.6sec clear of the BRM, which was hampered by suspension problems according to Quentin Spurring's *Autosport* race report. Rindt in his last race finished third in heat one and first in heat two, although Surtees won on aggregate by 3.4sec, whilst the day's fastest lap was posted by Jackie Stewart in the new Tyrrell in its first race, before it retired. Oliver rounds Lodge Corner with the impressive-looking Lodge in the background and its magnificent trees. In the 18th century it was an estate that had originally included a Tudor house reportedly destroyed by fire, rebuilt in baroque style by John Egerton with ornamental gardens, amidst farmland, with some of the buildings designed by Joseph Turner. This too was destroyed by fire in 1926, and then bombed in 1940 during the Second World War.

The 1970 Italian GP will forever be associated with the death of Jochen Rindt and the possible failure of the right-hand front brake shaft of his Lotus 72, as chief mechanic Dick Scammell believes. However, it was suggested by the late Peter Warr (who had joined Lotus in 1969) talking to Simon Taylor in *Motor Sport*, that the wingless 72 (for extra straight-line speed) had too much rear brake bias and had gone out of control under heavy braking for the Parabolica, the shaft braking under the high-speed impact with the Armco. This was exacerbated by the rear left Firestone tyre being of a harder compound to accommodate Monza's largely right-hand corners. Colin Chapman wrote a detailed letter, published in *Autosport* on 24 September 1970, the gist of which was that the brake shaft failure suffered by John Miles at the Österreichring was different and could not comment further until the wreckage of the car was released by the Monza authorities. Here Rindt talks to Chapman by the Lotus transporter in the Monza paddock. Karl Jochen Rindt (28 April 1942 – 5 September 1970) was German born but raised by his grandparents in Graz, Austria, after his parents were killed in an Allied bombing raid on Hamburg during the Second World War.

↑ Anybody who still doubts Jackie Stewart's status as the era's greatest F1 driver should study this stunning David Phipps image as Jackie grapples with the Tyrrell March 701/4-2. Ongoing fuel feed problems with the embryonic Tyrrell 001 meant that Stewart drove the March for one last time in a race, and after witnessing Rindt's corpse and crying in the cockpit he set off to record third fastest time. Note that the March is entirely bereft of any aerodynamic aids, and the skill, not to mention bravery, required to do this at high speed cannot be articulated by mere platitudes. Stewart finished second at Monza having led the race at various times, 5.73sec behind Regazzoni's victorious Ferrari.

⬆ Rob Walker had taken delivery of his Lotus 72 preceding the Oulton Park Gold Cup where it lasted three laps of heat one, setting a precedent for this unfortunate car. It was John Miles's chassis R1 that had been updated and renumbered. At Monza all the 72s were withdrawn following Rindt's accident, and afterwards Rob Walker had the car's front brake shafts crack tested by Vickers Armstrong. They described the front shafts as shattered, telling Rob that they could have failed at any time over the next few laps at Monza. The car was back for the Canadian GP at St Jovite, but Graham Hill started last after the Lotus caught fire and its clutch disintegrated during practice. The race brought gearbox problems and a loose rear wishbone mounting, leaving Hill 13 laps adrift. Here he is followed by Jack Brabham, also having a very bad weekend, with Stommelen's 'German' BT33, Eaton's BRM, and Schenken's de Tomaso following on. The race was dominated by Stewart's Tyrrell until it broke a front stub axle, leaving Ickx's Ferrari to win, a hat trick for Maranello, which was also the eighth consecutive GP win for Firestone tyres.

→ The US GP at Watkins Glen was the penultimate GP of 1970 and it was the final time for the track in its 2.3-mile form, which had been partially resurfaced following a Can-Am race in July. Meanwhile, the 1 October 1970 edition of *Autosport* confirmed that John Miles had left Gold Leaf Team Lotus to be replaced by Swedish F3 and F5000 racer Reine Wisell. In the pits Wisell and Chapman look on whilst a wrapped-up Maria-Helena Fittipaldi smiles for the camera, with Reine's green helmet in the foreground. Fittipaldi went on to win the race in only his fourth GP start, and Wisell finished third, which was to be his best-ever GP result. However, the victory was fortuitous as Jacky Ickx's Ferrari started from pole position, but it was Jackie Stewart who led the race for 82 laps until his engine broke, having lapped most of the field including the eventual winner. The Belgian followed Pedro Rodriguez for 15 laps before taking over second place, where he stayed until lap 56 when he pitted with a broken fuel line which dropped him to 12th place. Jacky eventually climbed back to fourth place, setting a new lap record three laps from the end, and but for the pit stop he would have won the race, and following Mexico, the World Championship.

→ Back then some grands prix attracted 'local' stars, usually running last season's cars, thus Gus Hutchison at Watkins Glen in his Brabham BT26A/3 which had begun its racing life as Jochen Rindt's Repco-powered mount at the 1968 Oulton Park Gold Cup. Like all the BT26s it had been updated for 1969 with a Cosworth DFV motor and Ickx won with it at Oulton Park and the Canadian GP, finishing off in second place in Mexico before it passed to Hutchison to finish second at Sebring in December. He then raced it during 1970 in Canada and America, winning twice back-to-back at Sears Point and Dallas International Speedway. For the 1967 SCCA Formula A champion, Watkins Glen was his only GP start and the car's final World Championship appearance. He qualified on the penultimate row and lasted 22 laps before one of the Brabham's auxiliary fuel tanks came adrift. The following car is Peter Gethin's McLaren M14A/1, which finished a delayed 14th and last.

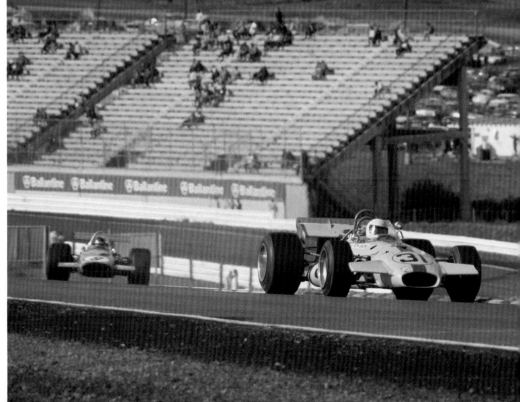

The last GP of the season at Mexico City was something of an anti-climax, with the championship already decided at Watkins Glen. Additionally, the event was funded by 'starting money', which meant that the already jaded teams had to pay for transporting their cars, personnel, and equipment from Watkins Glen to Mexico City and back to New York post race. So only 18 cars attended the race at the renamed Ricardo Rodriguez circuit near to Mexico City, which *Autosport's* photographer and race reporter David Phipps reckoned could become the smog capital of the world. During practice Jack Brabham is holding the Goodyear tyre temperature check card, with Mr Dennis again in shot. Brabham qualified fourth fastest and held third place for many laps before his engine blew up with 13 laps to go. It was his final GP race as he had decided to retire, partly from family pressure, 15 years after his first World Championship start at Aintree in 1955.

Following the retirement of Johnny Servoz-Gavin during Monaco practice, Tyrrell raced just one car for Jackie Stewart at Spa, but at Zandvoort they introduced François Cevert who had been recommended by Stewart in 1969. The former French F3 champion and Tecno F2 racer qualified 15th at Zandvoort, but some were not impressed. *Autosport's* Patrick McNally commented that 'Somehow it is difficult to believe that Cevert will make the grade, though on this occasion he was ahead of pretty impressive company.' By season's end Cevert had one points-scoring finish (sixth at Monza) but at Mexico he only lasted a few laps before his engine broke. The race was a Ferrari 1/2 for Ickx and Regazzoni, with Hulme's McLaren third. It was the last GP for Dunlop, whose tyres were used by BRM and Tyrrell in 1970, leaving Goodyear and Firestone to vie for supremacy. Franco Lini's picture of Cevert in the March 701/4 illustrates the aggression and determination that is almost invisible to the eye and lens in the near technological perfection of latter-day F1.

By 1970 the FIA and drivers had become far more safety conscious, but still races were allowed to run in potentially fatal circumstances. At the Mexican GP the spectators began to tear down the barriers during the support races and some threw bottles on to the circuit, which caused Jackie Stewart to plead with them to desist. The organisers were too frightened to cancel the race lest there were riots, and eventually after several sighting laps the GP was started some 75 minutes late. This is Reine Wisell in the GLTL Lotus 72C/R3, but note in the background that the track is lined by unprotected spectators. Especially the two on the right who are evidently oblivious to what is going on as they examine a magazine or perhaps the race programme. Fortunately nobody died as a result of this stupidity. The Mexican GP had started as a non-championship race in 1962, and following the 1970 race did not return to the World Championship calendar until 1986.

NEVER IN DOUBT

Nobody could challenge Jackie Stewart's brilliance with Derek Gardner's Tyrrell 001/003 in 1971. Stewart won six GPs and the drivers' championship by a huge margin from Ronnie Peterson in the March 711 (no wins but four second places). March had bounced back from the disappointing 701 but it was more driver than car whilst Tyrrell No. 2 Cevert won the US GP. Meanwhile messrs Ickx, Regazzoni and part-timer Mario Andretti managed only two wins between them for Maranello, the cars were very fast but chronically unreliable. BRM won the Austrian GP (Siffert) and Italian GP (Gethin) GPs but lost both Pedro Rodriguez who was killed racing a Ferrari in an Interserie race in Germany and Jo Siffert at the end of season Brands Hatch Victory Race. The team never fully recovered. Lotus and their relatively inexperienced drivers struggled during 1971, made worse by Fittipaldi's debilitating injuries from a road accident in France. They also experimented with the gas turbine 56B to their detriment. McLaren were still missing Bruce and their new M19 was proving problematical. Brabham employed Graham Hill and Tim Schenken but despite his Silverstone Trophy win Hill suffered numerous mechanical problems, his variable form notwithstanding, and Schenken proved better than the machinery. Chris Amon and Jean-Pierre Beltoise were Matra mounted but results were disappointing and the latter faced a temporary ban. Racer turned team owner/constructor John Surtees won the Oulton Park Gold Cup in his new car but the rest were racing for places only whilst the first slick tyres made their bow in Spain.

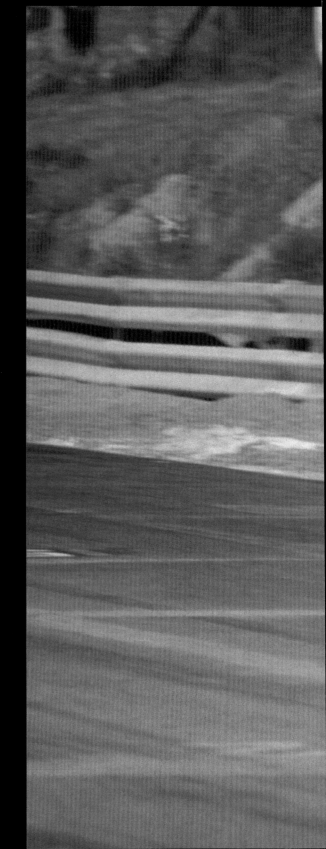

⬇ Despite the lucky win at Watkins Glen in 1970 following Jochen Rindt's fatal accident at Monza, GLTL lost momentum during 1971. This was hardly surprising given their drivers' relative lack of F1 experience and other problems, as noted elsewhere, which ultimately resulted in an admonitory dressing down from the boss at Paul Ricard. At the Canadian GP, Mosport, Fittipaldi and Wisell lined up fourth and seventh. Emerson wanted a full soft set-up for the race but Chapman compromised with more rear wing and softer damper settings. This resulted in Wisell finishing fifth and Fittipaldi fading to seventh, and 1971 was to be the first time since 1959 that Lotus failed to win a World Championship GP. Here we see 'Emmo' pressing on in chassis 72/5, displaying a touch of oversteer.

◀ One year on and March introduced their new 711, which was Cosworth DFV or Alfa Romeo V8-powered. The Robin Herd-designed car had substantial input from Frank Costin and ex-Lotus man Geoff Ferris. This is the impressive-looking Alfa-powered version showing its later-to-be-discarded inboard front brakes with no front aerofoils. As with McLaren in 1970, the Italian motor was not a success, and neither Andrea de Adamich (who had driven the similarly powered McLaren M14D in 1970 to no great effect) nor Nanni Galli troubled friend or foe during 1971. In the car park we can see two Minis, an MG Midget/Austin Healey Sprite, and a VW Beetle, with Robin Herd in the background with hands in pockets, whilst nearer to camera are *Autosport*'s John Bolster and what looks like Max Mosley in a formal suit.

◀ The usual game of musical chairs had taken place in European F1 over the winter, and when the circus reassembled at Kyalami in early March there were 25 starters for the South African GP. One major change was Mario Andretti joining Ferrari on a part-time basis following the death of Ignazio Giunti, and he duly won the race from pole sitter Jackie Stewart in the Tyrrell 001. Regazzoni finished third with a misfiring Ferrari having led for 16 laps before Hulme took the lead until six laps from the end when a bolt dropped out of a rear upper radius arm and Denny just crawled round to finish. In his *Autosport* column 'Behind the Wheel', Denny wrote, 'I knew I was going to have some problems with SuperWop … but it was going to be my race.' Imagine writing that now, the thought police would be on your doorstep at 4am. So Andretti in 312B1/02 beat Jackie by 20.9sec, the Tyrrell allegedly handicapped by a less potent race engine than its practice counterpart.

⬆ After the sun and hospitality of Kyalami the conditions at Brands Hatch for the sixth Race of Champions (a non-championship event) on a late March weekend were suitably grey and discouraging. Clay Regazzoni sits in the new Ferrari 312B2/005 with its wider, flatter, wedge nose and new rear suspension as an admiring public look on. He had crashed the car heavily during Kyalami practice and a complete front-end rebuild was required for Brands. On a damp track only Regazzoni and Graham Hill (debuting the new Brabham BT34) opted for 'dry' tyres rather than intermediates, and even though Stewart's Tyrrell led for 25 laps he was no match for the Ferrari on the drying track. Hill, meanwhile, made his way to third place, but before he could pass Stewart the BT34's tired motor failed, whilst the other front runner Denny Hulme (McLaren M19A) retired because of a misfire, leaving John Surtees a distant third behind Stewart. Clay's buttoned tartan flat cap was very much the fashion at this time.

Frank Williams entered two Marches at Brands, his new 711 for Ronnie Peterson and this 701/6, which Henri Pescarolo had raced at Kyalami. Brands supremo John Webb persuaded Frank to let Ray Allen, who had won the very first Formula Ford race at Brands Hatch on 12 July 1967, drive it. Allen, like so many British racers of the period, lacked the backing to progress much further up the ladder (he also raced in F5000) and here he finished a respectable sixth in an outdated car that he had never driven before, which has had its side-mounted aerofoil/fuel tanks removed.

→ One week later F1 arrived at the Ontario Motor Speedway in California for the non-championship Questor GP. There were 18 F1 cars, including Ferrari, and 15 Formula A cars (American equivalent of F5000) driven by Mark Donohue, Peter Revson, Sam Posey, et al. Franco Lini captures some of the drivers in repose pre-race. From left to right: Graham Hill, Tim Schenken and Ronnie Peterson with appropriately leggy, long-haired girl, and standing Jo Siffert, Henri Pescarolo, Jacky Ickx with Howden Ganley and Reine Wisell. At far left American actor and racing enthusiast James Garner is carrying a much-signed Bell Star helmet. This was the only race for F1 cars held here, which attracted a crowd of 55,000, a disappointment by American standards. However, *Autosport* of 1 April 1971 reported that the FIA had accepted the Speedway's application for a round of the World Championship in April 1972, which would have meant two US GPs that year. It was not to be. Questor was the name of the holding company with diverse interests, and much money was expended in making things perfect. However, by the late 1970s there were operating problems and the OMS bonds had fallen dramatically in value whilst land prices had risen from 1971 values of $7,500 to $150,000 per acre by 1980. Chevron Land Company, a subsidiary of Chevron Oil, acquired a majority of the bonds, thereafter purchasing the land, and the track was demolished in 1980 at a cost of US $3m. They paid US $10m for it against a commercial real estate development value of US $120m at the time.

→ An impassive-looking Henri Pescarolo in Frank Williams's smart, dark blue March 711/3 with its trademark March tea tray front wing awaits the action. Behind is Chris Amon's Matra MS120B/4 with his helmet perched on the nose of the car as Chris walks by in the background. 'Pesca' qualified mid-field but had a collision with Schenken's Brabham in heat one which resulted in retirement. In heat two the patched-up repair broke and the March was out again. This shot clearly shows the influence of Frank Costin's aerodynamic theories, his reasoning being that you could not extract another 15bhp from the DFV (in period) but you could gain the equivalent in drag reduction. He was mistaken. The orange Union 76 ball decals on either side of the 711's nose represent the then El Segundo-based Union Oil which introduced their '76' gasoline in 1932, the figure relating to the octane rating at this time and also to the American Spirit of 76. Today the brand is owned by ConocoPhillips, whilst the 76 ball has become a minor design icon over the decades. Williams also entered the March 701/6 that Ray Allen had driven at the ROC, for Derek Bell to no great effect. Mario Andretti (Ferrari) won the two-heat event on aggregate from Jackie Stewart's Tyrrell and Denny Hulme's McLaren.

In an age where F1 cars are restricted to World Championship outings only, note the schedule for many of the teams during the first few months of 1971. It began with Buenos Aires on 24 January for a non-championship race, followed by the South African GP at Kyalami on 6 March, Brands Hatch on 21 March for the ROC, before pitching up at the Questor GP in California on 28 March and back across the Atlantic for the Rothmans/Daily Express International Spring Trophy at Oulton Park on 9 April. Nine days after this came the Spanish GP. Montjuich Park near Barcelona was a longer, faster version of Monaco (2.36 miles/3.79km), which provided an impressive historic architectural backdrop with suitably primitive paddock conditions. Ferrari entered three 312Bs now producing 460bhp at 12,400rpm for Mario Andretti (No. 6 chassis 002), Clay Regazzoni (No. 5 chassis 004), and beyond Jacky Ickx's 003. They also brought as a training car the B2/005 that won the Brands Hatch Race of Champions.

Just beyond the Ferraris was Team Surtees with their Brooke Bond Oxo Rob Walker transporter, and at top left is Rob Walker with legendary photographer Geoff Goddard beside the transporter's open door. Brooke Bond Oxo had sponsored Rob Walker in his last season as an entrant in 1970 and had moved to Team Surtees for 1971. Two TS9s were entered, the nearest to the camera being Rolf Stommelen's *Auto Motor und Sport-Eifelland*-sponsored chassis 002 (as *Auto Motor* had done with Brabham in 1970) making its first appearance, whilst Surtees's chassis 01 rests behind. There is more grass here than on the Ferrari patch but the machinery/transporter aside this looks like a scene from a British hill climb paddock. It was a miserable weekend for the team, with Stommelen and Surtees qualifying 19th and 22nd (last) because of assorted woes, and in the race they both dropped out.

The front cover of *Autosport* 22 April 1971 was headed 'Stewart beats the 12-cyl challenge in Spanish GP'. Given the results thus far during 1971, the apparent neurosis about the Cosworth DFV being superseded by the V12 brigade, which had begun in 1970, was understandable. Ickx and Regazzoni shared the front row with Amon's Matra, with Stewart's Tyrrell and Rodriguez's BRM on the second row, so it was four V12s versus one Cosworth DFV. However, Stewart won by 3.4sec (his third successive Spanish GP victory) in the new Tyrrell 003 with its modified suspension to suit the new low-profile 'slicks' (their first usage in a GP) from Ickx who set fastest lap in the closing stages. Amon finished third, whilst Andretti and Regazzoni both retired. Here Stewart leads one of the Ferraris, possibly Regazzoni, on the anti-clockwise circuit. He is looking over to his left, perhaps having spotted the child in what is surely a restricted area out accelerating him on the other side of the Armco. Who are you?

By 1971 Graham Hill was in better shape having joined Brabham, but assorted car problems and unreliability during both practice and race had undermined his form. The unique Ron Tauranac-designed 'lobster claw' BT34 (the two radiators were placed in separate nacelles either side of the front aerofoil) had shown well at its Brands Hatch debut until it retired, and then it broke again at the Questor GP. However, at the two-heat GEN/Daily Express International Trophy on 8 May 1971 it held together (or rather the engine did) to give Graham one last F1 victory. In heat one he finished third behind Stewart's winning Tyrrell and the Rodriguez BRM, but in heat two Stewart crashed on lap one at Copse because of a sticking throttle, leaving Hill to catch and overtake the BRM (which had a puncture) and go on to win. As Graham rushes towards Geoff Goddard's camera on a wet track during practice one is reminded of just how softly sprung period F1 cars were in modern terms.

The Automobil Club de Monaco's insistence on limiting race starters to 18 rather than the 20 imposed by the Geneva agreement, which the ACM had not signed up to, had disastrous consequences for Ferrari and Mario Andretti. Two of the three practice sessions were wet and when Andretti's Ferrari broke down in the second, dry session, Mario was out. The French V12s were also suffering here. This is Jean-Pierre Beltoise at Mirabeau in the Matra MS120B/5, who ran as high as sixth at Monaco before a crown wheel and pinion failure on lap 48, two laps after Amon retired with the same problem. Matra blamed the lighter Hewland FG300 transmission, but whatever the reason it was a shame for the French team given the venue. Beltoise, meanwhile, was racing under a shadow following the Giunti tragedy at Buenos Aires and he was subsequently suspended from racing after the British GP until the Canadian GP in October.

⇨ Looking down on Ronnie Peterson in the March 711/02 as he races to second place at Monaco, 25sec behind yet another Jackie Stewart triumph, and what a triumph it was. The Tyrrell's rear brake balance bar had shifted before the start and could not be adjusted in time, so he won the race with no rear brakes. Peterson qualified on the fourth row despite having to abandon new ventilated front disc brakes, and rose through the field, eventually passing the Siffert/Ickx duel to claim second place on lap 31, where he stayed until the end of the race. This is the chicane as it was, a scary high-speed left, right flick with no room for error, whilst the spectators look on from their balconies, and others from a makeshift grandstand behind the barriers as an ocean liner rests in the bay. It was a big day for March, but as Robin Herd recalled in Mike Lawrence's *The Story of March: Four Guys and a Telephone*, 'It was very poignant because on the day March turned the corner, when Ronnie came second at Monaco, Graham Coaker died.' Coaker had been one of the original founders of March and died from septicaemia caused by complications from a broken leg after crashing his March 712 (a leaving present from March) in a Formula Libre race at Silverstone on 12 April 1971.

Gold Leaf Team Lotus came to Zandvoort with two 72s plus the gas turbine 56B, which was ultimately driven by the team's F3 star, Australian Dave Walker, but no Emerson Fittipaldi. Following his F2 win at the Whit Monday Crystal Palace event and en route to his new abode in Lausanne, Emerson had a serious road accident near Dijon. This left him with a fractured sternum and broken ribs, whilst his pregnant wife suffered a broken jaw and facial injuries. The incident and its severity were played down at the time and Emerson missed the Dutch GP. Problems arose when Walker, awaiting an engine repair on the 56B, drove Fittipaldi's car (which was supposed to be raced by Dave Charlton if Walker drove the 56B), and crashed it. This left Walker with the repaired 56B and Charlton without a drive. The race was just as fraught, with Walker going off the road on lap six and Wisell stopping just beyond the pit lane exit with a loose rear wheel, having been in fifth. Unwilling to risk driving the car a full lap back to the pits he reversed up the pit lane where the wheel was reaffixed, but he was subsequently disqualified.

Gijs van Lennep's F1 career began at Zandvoort in 1971 driving the third Team Surtees car, the original but updated TS7/001 that was hired out to Stichting Autoraces Nederland. He started on the penultimate row with a respectable time, given the relative uncompetitiveness of the older car and his lack of F1 experience. However, thanks in part to his Firestone tyres, van Lennep drove an impressive race eventually finishing eighth. He looks rather serious here, no doubt wondering how he is going to fare. The race was dominated by the Firestone-shod cars, specifically the V12s, which were easier to drive in the conditions, of Ickx (Ferrari) and Rodriguez (BRM), with Regazzoni third, a lap behind. Everybody else was lapped at least twice or more.

Following two years at Clermont Ferrand, the French GP moved to the new 3.6-mile (5.8km) Paul Ricard circuit near Bandol in the south of France, a stark contrast to the rugged Charade circuit in the Auvergne. Ongoing fears that Maranello's potent V12 might ultimately overwhelm the Cosworth DFV were misplaced. Tyrrell's engines were superior here (perhaps more so than any other DFVs) helped by a second-per-lap advantage in the dry, courtesy of Goodyear according to Patrick McNally in *Autosport*. Jackie Stewart (Tyrrell 003) led from start to finish (although he is lagging behind here), followed home by teammate Cevert, and Emerson Fittipaldi, who was still recovering from his road accident. Ickx (Ferrari 312B2/006 nearest camera) lasted only five laps before a probable crankshaft failure, whilst Regazzoni (Ferrari 312B/005) spun off on dropped oil and broke a wheel.

Jo Siffert finished fourth in the French GP in the BRM P160/02 just 3.1sec behind Fittipaldi's Lotus 72 after a long battle with the Brazilian. Following is sometime French FF champion and F3/F2 racer, Marseilles-born Max Jean (but known as Jean Max, allegedly after his name was reversed on a race entry), who hired Frank Williams's old March 701/6. He qualified last but one and finished last in the thoroughly uncompetitive car after delays, whilst in front of him was Parisian François Mazet who qualified last in another old March, this being Jo Siffert's 701/05 that he had raced so unsuccessfully in 1970. It was the only World Championship start for the French duo, wasted on obsolete machinery. Meanwhile, the French GP was the final F1 race for Siffert's teammate Pedro Rodriguez who raced second to Jackie Stewart in the French GP until a coil failure ended his race on lap 28. Pedro suffered a fatal crash driving Herbert Müller's Ferrari 512M in an Interserie race at the Norisring on 11 July 1971.

The talented South African Dave Charlton came a very long way to drive a Lotus 72 at Zandvoort, which did not materialise, but at the British GP he had the car, whilst Wisell was put into the 56B turbine that had been raced in Holland by Lotus F3 star Dave Walker. It was not a successful outing with 72D/R3, as first an oil union failed and then he missed the final practice session whilst the engine mountings were strengthened following a failure on Fittipaldi's car. Then a piston failed on the warm-up lap and Charlton managed one slow lap before retiring to the pits, almost colliding with Hill's crippled Brabham BT34 that had been hit by Oliver's McLaren at the start. The unhappy faces on the grid tell a tale, whilst behind the Lotus three girls in 'hot pants', one wearing the GLTL brand, the other two promoting Dave Walker, are simply enjoying the sunny day and the atmosphere of a grand prix.

↑ BRM were still fielding their old P153s during 1971/72, and this is Howden Ganley in chassis 06 at Silverstone, where he finished eighth. Ganley had made his GP debut at Kyalami and he stayed until the end of 1972 with the Bourne team, with whom he scored his best GP results, two fourth-place finishes in the 1971 US GP and the 1972 German GP. Once again we can see how softly sprung the GP cars were in this era, and how much more they moved about. The race was another Jackie Stewart triumph, with Peterson second again for March (shades of Monaco), and a still-suffering Emerson Fittipaldi a brave third.

↗ Following the death of Pedro Rodriguez, Louis Stanley employed Porsche sports car ace Vic Elford for the German GP. Elford had raced for Cooper in 1968 and then proved very competitive in Colin Crabbe's McLaren M7A in 1969 before running over the wreckage of Mario Andretti's crashed Lotus 63 at the German GP and suffering substantial arm and upper body injuries. Now he was back at the Nürburgring making a fleeting return to GP racing in what was to be his final F1 drive. 'Quick Vic' looks happy enough in BRM P160/01 but neither he nor Howden Ganley were competitive compared to team leader Jo Siffert, who qualified some 17sec quicker. At least Elford finished, albeit 11th, whilst the other two retired.

→ The German GP was Jackie Stewart's third consecutive GP victory, his fifth of the season thus far and the second 1/2 for Tyrrell. Clay Regazzoni finished third, with part-time Ferrari racer Mario Andretti fourth, hampered by handling problems. Jacky Ickx had briefly led the race but could not hold Stewart, and then crashed at Wipperman on lap two, ending his race. Once again Siffert impressed, taking second place on lap two, but coil failure (again) ended his race, although having taken a short cut to reach the pits he would have been disqualified anyway. Additionally, a lower wishbone mounting was tearing away from the monocoque, so retirement was inevitable. Instead of happy faces, Regazzoni, Stewart and Cevert, with accompanying officialdom and Helen Stewart, all look rather sombre.

A week before the Austrian GP, Matra withdrew from the race citing handling problems apparently caused by the engine lacking rigidity as a suspension mounting point. The competition was going faster and faster and Matra were getting slower as the season progressed. Additionally, Jean-Pierre Beltoise was temporarily banned, so the French team decided to use the time before Monza to rebuild the cars. Meanwhile, at McLaren Peter Gethin had left for BRM, which promoted Jackie Oliver into the original M19A/1, seen here as team principal Teddy Meyer converses with Phil Kerr under the awning in the Österreichring paddock. Patrick McNally's race report in *Autosport* noted, 'McLaren once again had trouble with their transporter, and Oliver's car plus many of the spares only arrived in time for the final practice session on Saturday.' So Oliver started last, his M19 using M14 rear suspension, and finished ninth, whilst Hulme's newer car survived but six laps before the engine self-destructed. Alongside the McLaren transporter is the Clarke Mordaunt-Guthrie wagon for Mike Beuttler's March 711.

The Austrian GP was a well deserved victory for Jo Siffert in the BRM P160/03 who started from pole position and led the race from start to finish. He left behind Stewart's Tyrrell that had developed serious vibrations and understeer, the Scotsman finally waving through his teammate Cevert on lap 21. Stewart then lost a rear wheel on lap 36, whilst the second Tyrrell developed gearbox troubles and blew up, leaving Fittipaldi in second place. However, with Ickx's Ferrari retiring, Jackie was the 1971 F1 World Champion. As the race drew to a close Siffert began to lose pace and was rapidly being caught by Fittipaldi's Lotus 72, his lead shrinking from 24sec to just 4.12sec at the flag. It transpired that 'Seppi' had been nursing a punctured tyre for the final 12 laps. BRM, or perhaps more accurately Louis Stanley, entered five cars here (including a spare P160) and some, Siffert amongst them, thought this was too much.

⬆ It was a strange race at Monza with no Gold Leaf Team Lotus (they actually appeared as World Wide Racing, a familiar alias, with the gas turbine 56B for Fittipaldi) or Denny Hulme and the McLaren M19s. The former because of the continuing threat of legal action over Rindt's 1970 crash, the latter having decided to ship their newer cars to Canada for the next race. Even so, despite the drivers' championship having been decided, the emotional hothouse of Monza promised a good race, and so it was. In the pits following his recent Oulton Park Gold Cup victory is John Surtees and his new Surtees TS9/005. 'Big John' pulls on his gloves, while Rob Walker is behind the TS9 with its new nose and rear-mounted radiators, and beyond Rolf Stommelen in the German-sponsored TS9/001. Unfortunately, 005 was overheating and the rear-mounted rads were abandoned, the car reverting to its orthodox cooling. *Autosport* noted that Surtees spent more time running the team than driving. John lasted but a few laps before his 11-series Cosworth broke, whilst Stommelen non-started after a high-speed accident when a tyre came off its rim.

↗ Having non-started at the 1966 German GP, Silvio Moser's F1 championship career proper began in 1967 at the British GP where he drove a Cooper-ATS confection for Charles Vögele. In 1970 he contracted Italian F3 constructor Vittorio Bellasi to build him a Cosworth DFV-powered car. It was large, heavy, and uncompetitive with suspension based upon the Brabham BT24, and made its debut at the Dutch GP where Moser failed to qualify, as he did at the French, German, and Italian GPs. However, Silvio did manage to make the start in Austria, only to retire. A year passed and Moser, in Bellasi-Ford, made it on to the grid at Monza, albeit on the penultimate row, and the recalcitrant machine was soon out with a broken shock absorber mounting. This was its final GP outing but it should be noted that Silvio had won the Saint Ursanne-les-Rangiers European Championship hill climb and the Kerenzerberg hill climb in 1970 with it, whilst Gildo Guidi finished second in the Oberhallau hill climb in 1971.

➡ In this order: Regazzoni (Ferrari), Peterson (March), Stewart (Tyrrell), Cevert (Tyrrell), Hailwood (Surtees), Siffert (BRM), Amon (Matra), and Gethin (BRM) all took turns to lead the Italian GP at one point or another. Of these, Peterson led the most (21 laps) whilst eventual winner Peter Gethin led across the line only three times, first on lap 52, and started the final (55th) lap in fourth place. A banzai effort at Parabolica saw Gethin (who had been using 12,000rpm rather than the official limit of 11,200) slip between Peterson and Cevert to win the race by 0.01sec, with Cevert 0.08sec behind the Swede, then Hailwood another 0.09sec behind, and Ganley a further 0.43sec back. In all just 0.61sec covered the first five cars and it was to remain the fastest ever GP for decades thereafter. Peter races on in the elegant BRM P160/01 to a famous victory. Peter Kenneth Gethin, 21 February 1940 – 5 December 2011.

▣ Mosport Park, near Ontario, hosted the 1971 Canadian GP, and Roger Penske with Philadelphia Ferrari-dealer Kirk F. White were running the McLaren M19A/1 for Mark Donohue. Practice was dry and Donohue lined up eighth on the grid. The race, however, was wet and Donohue drove brilliantly to finish third ahead of Hulme's newer M19, which finished fourth. Even so, he was not impressed with the car and its 'rising rate' suspension, especially at the rear, but Doug Nye noted in *McLaren: The Grand Prix, Can-Am and Indy Cars* that 'Donohue later came to believe that the M19's basic problem had more to do with poor wing forms than trick suspension. …' The shortened race was won by Jackie Stewart (his sixth championship win of the season) after battling with Ronnie Peterson's March 711 for much of the time. The Swede led for 12 laps but a collision when lapping Eaton's BRM damaged the 711's front wing and also caused braking problems, so Peterson finished second when he might just have won. Penske (right) and his legendary driver Mark Donohue, who was making his F1 debut here, are looking at the BRM opposition before the race.

◄ One of the lucky recipients of the two non-starters at Mosport was VW-dealer Pete Lovely who ran this hybrid Lotus based upon an ex-Graham Hill 69 F2 car with the back end of Pete's 49/R11. Ultimately the cars were rebuilt to their original state. Regardless of all else, this was an uncompetitive machine, not helped by the fact that it retained its F2 front brakes. He finished last but unclassified nine laps down. Gerard Carlton 'Pete' Lovely 11 April 1926 – 15 May 2011.

▲ The final race in the World Championship F1 calendar was the US GP at the now-lengthened Watkins Glen (from 2.3 to 3.3777 miles/5.44km) on 3 October 1971. It had four new corners and was first used for a Can-Am race in July, the idea being to have a projected lap time of 100sec, which was calculated by computer models and proved reasonably accurate with Stewart setting a pole time of 102.645sec. This is Denny Hulme's McLaren M19A/2 in the pits, looking strange with an experimental full-width nose. Denny started from the front row but his car had an out-of-balance wheel and he lost ground before pitting on lap 32 to change all four wheels, although it made no difference as Hulme crashed on lap 48. The omnipresent Alastair Caldwell, in matching orange shirt and 'shades', looks on with the boss, Teddy Meyer, to his right.

◄ This is Chris Craft, renowned sports and saloon car ace who was racing Jack Brabham's 1970 Brabham BT33/2 at Watkins Glen. It was entered by Ecurie Evergreen (aka Alain de Cadanet and David Weir) and managed by former racer Keith Greene, whose father was Sid Greene of Gilby Engineering. They had already contested the Oulton Park Gold Cup and the Canadian GP, although non-started at Mosport Park because of engine problems. Decades later, Alain told the author that he did not care for F1 and Watkins Glen was their final outing with the Brabham, the engine of which was used in de Cadanet's Gordon Murray-designed Duckhams Special at Le Mans 1972. Craft's race was terminated by a broken rear cross member according to Alan Phillip's race data in *Autosport*.

◄ Jackie Stewart's race at Watkins Glen was severely compromised by tyre problems that allowed teammate Cevert to win the GP in Tyrrell 002. This was in some ways a justification of the Frenchman's F1 career – he had not been highly rated by some when he joined Tyrrell in 1970. Even then, over four decades ago, there was pressure to perform too soon, and all the more demanding when the other car was being driven by the world's best F1 racer. The handsome, smiling Frenchman receives his reward, which was both ironic and tragic as this was to be Cevert's only GP win and the scene of his fatal practice crash two years later. Jo Siffert finished second for BRM in what was his last GP, and Ronnie Peterson signed off his impressive year with third for March, which made him runner-up in the World Championship.

⬆ Despite its full-width nose, Tim Schenken's Brabham BT33/3 looks more 1960s than early 1970s, the illusion enhanced by the virtual absence of visible sponsorship. The Australian had impressed, even though the team suffered many mechanical failures and woes during 1971, Tim finishing sixth in Germany and an outstanding third in Austria. However, the rest of his season and that of Graham Hill, bar the International Trophy victory and a fifth in Austria, was a disappointment. Schenken rounds Druids during practice for the Rothmans World Championship Victory Race at Brands Hatch on 24 October 1971 in which he recorded equal seventh fastest time with Jackie Stewart and finished fifth. The race result was decided on the order at the end of lap 14 following Jo Siffert's fatal accident, which gave victory to Peter Gethin just ahead of Emerson Fittipaldi, with Stewart third and the already deceased Siffert fourth.

1972

SAME ENGINE, BUT DIFFERENT TEAM

A rapidly maturing Emerson Fittipaldi in the now John Player Special Lotus 72 ended up winning five GPs and the World Championship. The Lotus No. 2 Dave Walker's F1 career was doomed with every problem imaginable and so it proved. Jackie Stewart won four GPs, but his impossibly demanding transatlantic work schedule during 1971 left him with debilitating medical problems and he missed the Belgian GP. Teammate Cevert managed two second place finishes and a fourth in an otherwise unsatisfactory season. Only McLaren, BRM and Ferrari disrupted the Lotus/Tyrrell hegemony winning at Kyalami (Hulme) Monaco (Beltoise for BRM's final GP victory) and the Nürburgring (Ickx, unbelievably his last GP win). Ferrari were as rapid as ever but unreliable whilst perennially unlucky Chris Amon should have won the French GP but suffered a puncture and ended up third for Matra. The French team were only running Amon and both driver and team deserved better. Meanwhile attempts by the CSI to impose compulsory refuelling for GPs without prior consultation caused much consternation in the ranks but ultimately bureaucracy was forced to back down, fortunately. By now the teams (with exception) were more associated with their major sponsors rather than their historical entities. The rest were struggling including March who produced three different F1 cars in short order but some were biding their time awaiting better machinery, notably Brabham now owned by Bernie Ecclestone. They employed Carlos Reutemann and Wilson Fittipaldi whilst retaining Graham Hill who surprisingly ended up their best scoring driver, albeit four points to Reutemann's three, which reflected their terminal reliability problems.

During 1971 Jackie Stewart had been driving for Tyrrell in F1, for Carl Haas in Can-Am, had attended numerous dinner and cocktail parties for Ford and Elf, made PR visits to American Goodyear tyre dealerships and public appearances in shopping malls for L&M cigarettes, which sponsored the Haas team. He also worked for ABC's *Wide World of Sports* programme, but the most punishing aspect was the constant transatlantic/long-haul flights to accommodate all this. Between 25 May and 31 October 1971 he made 18 such flights, with only a single week off. He was so exhausted that at the FIA annual presentation dinner in Paris, Helen had to accept on his behalf the award for being World Champion. She later persuaded Stewart to see a doctor in Geneva, who diagnosed a severe case of mononucleosis (glandular fever) and he was forced to rest over Christmas, but there would be further consequences during 1972. Nevertheless, Stewart (Tyrrell 003) led from start to finish in Buenos Aires, with Hulme (McLaren), and Ickx (Ferrari) trailing behind. The surprise of the weekend was the performance of Brabham's new signing, Carlos Reutemann, who put the unloved BT34 on pole. He briefly held second place before falling back with tyre problems, having chosen to race on the qualifying rubber, and ended up seventh after the inevitable stop for new rubber.

⬆ Now sporting the most famous sponsorship livery of this era, Colin Chapman's Lotus 72s arrived in Argentina for the first GP of 1972 as John Player Specials. Two were entered, one for Emerson Fittipaldi and this one, 72D/6. Following the travails of 1971, Reine Wisell was the sacrificial goat and he lost his Lotus drive to Australian Dave Walker. However, Reine, who had moved to BRM, was nevertheless to briefly race again for Lotus in 1972, as we shall see. Note the YPF fuel decal, which every car had to carry. Whilst Emerson qualified on the third row his teammate 'drove very sensibly' according to *Autosport*, sharing the penultimate row with Helmut Marko. Alas, the Australian was the victim of ingested sand and was disqualified for receiving outside assistance. This was a continuation of his various problems in F1, and things would not improve. Emerson, meanwhile, had got to within 2sec of leader Stewart in the race before the car began jumping out of fourth gear, but it ultimately retired with a broken radius arm. Michael Oliver, in his book *Lotus 72: Formula One Icon*, records that Fittipaldi had got so much traction off the start that it had bent both top radius arms, hence the failure.

→ These two are probably the best known of the local South African F1 drivers of this era, at least to Europeans. Their career records are too long to record here, and by 1972 John Love (left) was making his final GP start, in the Team Gunston Surtees TS9 in which he finished 16th after spinning off. He is best remembered for losing the 1967 South African GP after having to stop for fuel in his outdated Cooper-Climax T75 but still finishing second. John Maxwell Lineham Love, 7 December 1924 – 25 April 2005. The younger Dave Charlton (born 27 October 1936) retired his Lucky Strike Lotus 72 here in 1972, but he had first raced a Brabham in the 1967 race and, unlike Love, contested some European GPs in 1971/72, and finally ended his championship F1 career with a McLaren M23 in 1975.

➘ In 1970 he was Brabham-mounted, in 1971 Surtees, and for 1972 Rolf Stommelen drove for his sponsor Eifelland Caravans this March 721-4 (otherwise the Eifelland-Cosworth Type 21) with its bizarre-looking central periscope and scuttle-mounted intake, courtesy of artist Lutz Colani. However, it is still recognisably a 721, but by the Spanish GP it had acquired the later shovel-style nose. Subsequently, some of these cosmetic alterations would disappear. The car first appeared at Kyalami where Stommelen finished 13th, and here he is followed by Ganley's BRM P160B/04 that finished unclassified. He raced the car up to and including the Austrian GP, and out of eight GP starts his best results were two tenth places, after which he sold it to London Alfa Romeo- and BMW-dealer Hexagon of Highgate. They employed John Watson, who drove it on 6 September in the Players No. 6 Grand Prix at Phoenix Park, Ireland, but it retired, and then at the John Player Challenge Trophy, Brands Hatch, on 22 October, where Watson finished sixth, which seems to be its final period outing.

⬆ Still persevering with Brabham, or perhaps it was the other way round, Graham Hill out-qualified Reutemann's troubled BT34 at Kyalami (it had a seized rear roll bar). Graham survived a lively ride in the Brabham BT33/3 with fading brakes, having to pitch the car into oversteer entering corners. Despite this and the fitting of a new rev-limiter just before the start that lost him 700rpm, Hill finished a deserved sixth, just beating Niki Lauda's works March. Graham's continuing drive in the team was courtesy of Bernie Ecclestone, who had taken over Motor Racing Developments. At the front Denny Hulme made up for the disappointment of 1971 by winning the race (the M19A's only GP victory), despite overheating, from Emerson Fittipaldi and McLaren teammate Peter Revson, but it might have ended differently if Stewart's Tyrrell, which started from pole, set fastest race lap, and led, had not retired with gearbox failure.

↗ Peter Revson, like Mike Hailwood, was a returnee from the 1.5-litre F1 era, and had made a one-off appearance for Ken Tyrrell at Watkins Glen in 1971, but only lasted one lap because of clutch failure. He joined McLaren for 1972/73 and retired in Buenos Aires, finished third at Kyalami, and at Jarama started from row five and came in fifth on a circuit new to him. He is driving chassis M19A/2, whilst Hulme drove M19A/1 and led the race until his gearbox failed and he had to retire. Revson, like Andretti and Donohue before him, had prior American racing commitments, and when he was unavailable Brian Redman stood in for him at Monaco, Clermont Ferrand, Nürburgring, and Watkins Glen.

➡ Ferrari entered three of their 312B2s at Jarama, and here Andretti (005), Ickx (006), and Regazzoni (008) are in company with Cevert's Tyrrell 002. They finished, respectively, retired, second, and third, whilst Cevert also dropped out. The full-width nose had been used at Kyalami and retained in Spain, although the cars now had bigger rear wings, repositioned oil coolers and other detail changes, and Jacky Ickx was significantly faster than anybody else, starting from pole position. However, Lotus were now over their 1971 inconsistencies, or at least Fittipaldi was, and the Brazilian won the race convincingly in the JPS 72D.

◀ A troubled Jackie Stewart in Tyrrell 003 at Jarama. In his autobiography *Winning is Not Enough* Jackie Stewart wrote, 'Something was going wrong, and I was starting to go off the road more often than at any stage of my career. It was hard to tell whether the problem lay with the car or the driver.' Having spun off after being passed by Fittipaldi early in the Spanish GP, Stewart returned to Britain to test a McLaren at Goodwood with the intent of racing in the Can-Am series. However, he spun off twice, and then at the wet Monaco he pirouetted again but managed to finish fourth. Afterwards he complained to Helen about being constantly tired and seeing stars and floaters in his vision. A medical check-up in Lausanne revealed anaemia, and further investigation uncovered a duodenal ulcer. This ended his Can-Am aspirations and he was told to stop racing for six to eight weeks and was offered the choice of an operation or total rest, the former taking longer to recover from. He chose rest and missed the Belgian GP.

▲ Practice at Monaco was dry and sunny, and here Jean-Pierre Beltoise in the BRM P160B/01 awaits the action as the Monaco gendarme in his smart uniform looks on. Jean-Pierre qualified fourth fastest, but only one-tenth quicker than Peter Gethin in another P160. The race was, of course, very wet and Beltoise famously won his only GP, beating acknowledged wet-weather maestro Jacky Ickx by 38.2sec, and everybody else by a lap or considerably more. It was to be BRM's last World Championship win almost 13 years after Bonnier's Dutch GP triumph of 1959.

◄ Wilson Fittipaldi finished seventh in his first GP with MRD in Spain, and at Monaco he came in ninth with the Brabham BT33/3, which had been Hill's car, Graham having moved on to the new BT37. However, Wilson has the BT37-style nose on his older car and he finished ahead of an unhappy Hill whose car misbehaved during practice. Brian Redman, who finished fifth in the wet race, can be seen at 10 o'clock in Revson's M19A/2, the American being at Indianapolis.

⬆ Chris Amon was numero uno at Matra but their only regular driver for 1972. The V12 machine was now allegedly giving 450bhp at 11,500rpm (up from 440bhp). It had an altered nose with twin venting ducts and modified front suspension to accommodate the latest Goodyear rubber. Amon non-started at Buenos Aires because of various problems, and later some 77lb (35kg) was saved by the use of titanium exhausts and lighter rear wing and wheels. Nevertheless, instead of using the newer MS120C/06 at Monaco he went back to the older MS120B/04, which was adapted to take the modifications from chassis 06. Chris shared the third row with Gethin's BRM and went on to finish sixth, and here he negotiates the exit of Casino Square in the aquatic conditions.

This is Brazilian Carlos Pace, another of the South American F3 intake of 1970. He spent the season with Frank Williams, driving this old March 711/3, whilst teammate Henri Pescarolo endured the 721 and later the original Politoys FX3. Ron Tauranac, seen here in the Nivelles pits squatting by the March, had left MRD and was for a while acting as technical consultant for the team. Pace finished fifth in the Belgian GP, his best result, after which he failed to score any more points or finishes during 1972. The race fell to Fittipaldi's Lotus 72 ahead of Cevert's Tyrrell and Hulme's McLaren. There had been no Belgian GP in 1971, and in 1972 Nivelles-Baulers, near Brussels, hosted the race.

March's 1972 F1 campaign began with the 721 and then, for the Brands Hatch ROC, the 721X appeared for Ronnie Peterson. It made its championship debut at Jarama where both Niki Lauda and Ronnie Peterson retired. Aesthetically ugly and messy looking, it used an Alfa-based gearbox, and the entire engine/transmission lump was within the wheelbase, but the forward-biased weight distribution did not suit the Firestone rubber and the car displayed extremes of understeer and oversteer entering and exiting corners. Both cars finished at Monaco many laps behind, and at Nivelles Ronnie Peterson was ninth, two laps behind in chassis 721X/2 in its final race start. The 721 and 721X lasted but two GPs apiece before another variation, the F2-based 721G appeared at Clermont Ferrand for the factory team. However, one such car had already been built for Clarke-Mordaunt-Guthrie Racing and used by Mike Beuttler in Spain, where he failed to qualify.

→ The French GP was back at the Charade circuit near Clermont Ferrand for the fourth and final time in 1972 (1965/69/70/72). Practice and the race were led by Chris Amon in the Matra MS120D/07 until a puncture stopped him on lap 20. Thereafter he climbed back from eighth place to third at the flag, rapidly catching second-placed Emerson Fittipaldi. Another GP that Amon should have won but did not. So a recovering Jackie Stewart won the French GP for Tyrrell, whilst further down the field the team ran a third car for GP debutant Patrick Depailler. The Frenchman qualified 16th in Tyrrell 004 but two punctures, one of which is obvious here, dropped him out of contention and he finished last. Following this, Depailler raced to seventh in the US GP but subsequently did not return to F1 until 1974 with Tyrrell again. The Charade circuit was notable for its stony, dirt-ridden verges, and if you strayed off line too far this was the probable result, as poor Amon also discovered.

→ Marlboro's sponsorship of BRM in 1972 allowed Louis Stanley to continue his multi-car tactics, and in France five cars were entered. However, Gethin shunted his P160B during practice, and Beltoise's P160C broke a camshaft in unofficial practice on race day, so he took over Ganley's older car, which left three Bourne cars on the grid. Amidst these travails relative F1 rookie Helmut Marko in P160B-06 started an impressive sixth and harried Emerson Fittipaldi's Lotus 72 until tragically a stone thrown up by the Lotus on lap nine hit the Austrian's left eye, which left him with only right-eye vision. It was the end of his racing career. Here the BRM approaches the first corner pursued by Schenken's Surtees, and note that the P160's cockpit/screen surround seems to be askew.

⬆ Practice and the first 48 laps of the British GP were dominated by Ickx's Ferrari 312B2/005 from Stewart's Tyrrell 003 and Emerson Fittipaldi in the JPS Lotus 72D/R5. Then the Ferrari retired after many laps of fluctuating oil pressure caused by a leak, leaving the Tyrrell/Lotus duo contesting the lead, with Fittipaldi in front from lap 36 onwards to eventually win by 4.1sec. It was Emerson's third GP win of 1972 and by now the Lotus 72 was the faster car compared to the ageing Tyrrell 003 (the replacement 005 was not race ready), notwithstanding Stewart's health problems. The flag has dropped at precisely 2.30pm on 15 July 1972 on Brands Hatch's undulating pit straight, with Ickx leading away from Fittipaldi, a hidden Stewart, Hulme's McLaren M19C/1, the No. 11 BRM P160C of Beltoise that finished a delayed 11th, and the rest.

↗ At the end of 1970 Louis Stanley took BRM regular Jackie Oliver to dinner at the Dorchester where they discussed his drive for 1971. Jackie voiced concerns over a team member, which 'Big Lou' did not appreciate, it being somebody that he (Stanley) had confidence in, and subsequently Oliver received a letter terminating his contract. However, at Brands Hatch in 1972 Oliver was back in the team on a one-off basis following a late deal, leaving Wisell and Ganley temporarily displaced. Four BRMs had been entered, but Marlboro insisted on a three-car team that now consisted of Beltoise, Gethin, and Oliver. There were 26 starters and both Oliver and Gethin retired, the former with a rear suspension breakage on lap 37 and the latter with engine failure on lap six. This is Oliver in BRM P160B/05 leading GP newcomer Arturo Merzario in the second Ferrari 312B2/07 (Regazzoni was injured), into Druids. The Italian finished a worthy sixth and *Autosport* reported that he was awarded the BP Man of the Meeting and the newly instigated Marlboro Rouge et Blanc awards.

➡ Ferrari had become inconsistent, but the German GP was dominated by Jacky Ickx, who started from pole position and led all 14 laps, setting a new lap record 6.5sec quicker than Jackie Stewart's 1971 mark, and unbelievably it was his final GP victory. His teammate Clay Regazzoni finished a controversial second 48.3sec behind Ickx after he and Stewart touched wheels on the penultimate lap, resulting in the Scot spinning off. In picture, Regazzoni in Ferrari 312B2/07 leads Emerson Fittipaldi in Lotus 72D/R7 and Stewart still using Tyrrell 003. Of note was Fittipaldi's performance holding second place for six laps until he was forced out by a split gearbox casing that caused a brief fire.

⬆ Ken Tyrrell holds back Jackie Stewart in Tyrrell 005 at the Austrian GP, the new car at last in use and now sporting outboard front brakes after problems with the original inboard set-up. Emerson Fittipaldi in his regular Lotus 72D/R7 cruises by, but ultimately he used the T-car chassis R5 to set pole position at the Österreichring, whilst Stewart started from the second row. However, the Scot led for 23 laps before handling problems dropped him to an eventual seventh place. In the background Cevert pulls on his gloves, but he too was destined for a disappointing race, finishing ninth. Fittipaldi won in the T-car chassis R5 (race No. 31), but only just, from a closing Denny Hulme's McLaren, and he took one more step towards the 1972 World Championship.

↗ A trio of the greatest motor cycle racers of their time in the Monza pits, Giacomo Agostini fiddling with his pit pass, Mike Hailwood and 1964 F1 World Champion John Surtees. Hailwood is holding a copy of *Motoring News* 7 September 1972, which is headlining the victory of Muir/Miles in Malcom Gartlan's Ford Capri RS 2600 over the similar Ford Köln entries of Stewart/Cevert and Larrousse/Soler-Roig/Mass at the 6 Hours of Paul Ricard. More pertinently, underneath this the paragraph header reads Surtees duo dominates, a reference to the 1/2 victory of Hailwood and Carlos Pace in their Matchbox Team Surtees TS10s in the European championship for F2 drivers at Salzburg on 3 September. Monza was Team Patron John Surtees's last GP start but Hailwood would finish a F1 career best 2nd here, although he deserved better.

➡ During practice Niki Lauda leads Jacky Ickx, Clay Regazzoni, and Jackie Stewart, the Austrian using the front radiator, wide nose 721G-4 that Peterson had rejected in Austria. He qualified towards the rear of the field, but still in front of Peterson, who had engine problems in first practice and then an accident in the second session. Niki stopped after lap one to have grit removed from his throttle slides and rejoined last, where he stayed for the rest of the race five laps behind. Meanwhile, much had been and was happening backstage before, during, and post Monza. Peterson was going to Lotus, Regazzoni to BRM, Ganley to Williams, and Firestone announced they were pulling out of F1, but later changed their mind.

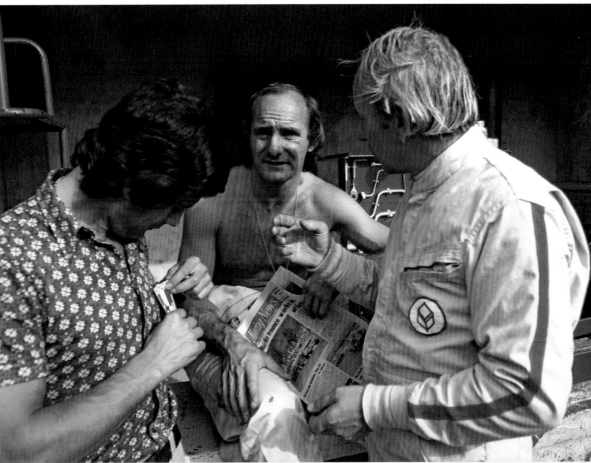

⬆ As the tension builds at Monza and adrenalin surges, the drivers await release. Amon (Matra MS120D-07) looks across at our photographer, and Ickx (Ferrari 312B2/05) on pole adjusts his helmet, with Stewart (Tyrrell 005) and Regazzoni (Ferrari 312B2/07 on the second row followed by Hulme (McLaren M19C/1), Fittipaldi (Lotus 72D/R5), and the rest. Ickx led for 45 laps before retiring with electrical trouble, or perhaps a fuel problem; Amon occupied third before retiring with fading brakes; Stewart travelled only a few yards before his clutch failed (because of a very high first gear installed for the chicanes); Regazzoni led but collided with Pace's March on lap 17; Hulme finished third, and Fittipaldi, having chased Ickx for many laps, won the race, his fifth GP win of the year, and with it the 1972 F1 World Championship. Lotus arrived at Monza concerned that the still ongoing Rindt inquiry might see the cars impounded and Colin Chapman in court, but all was well. Two cars (R5 and R7) were entered under World Wide Racing but came in separate transporters. The one carrying R7 was written off when a tyre burst near Milan en route to the race and the car was severely damaged. So Emerson used R5 (Dave Walker was not entered) and he endured a troubled practice as well as having to take the engine out of the damaged R7.

The penultimate GP of 1972 was in Canada at Mosport Park. Qualifying produced a McLaren 1/2 led by Peter Revson and Denny Hulme, with Ronnie Peterson's resurgent March occupying the front row. On the second row were Fittipaldi and Stewart with identical times. After four laps of the delayed fog-bound race Stewart assumed the lead and stayed there to win from Revson and Hulme, who was stuck behind Reutemann's Brabham until it ran out of fuel on the final lap. Further down the field, Tim Schenken in the Team Surtees TS9B-006 leads Reine Wisell in the JPS Lotus 72D/R6, the Australian heading for seventh place. The talented Schenken's season with Surtees yielded one fifth-place amongst six retirements and assorted no-point-scoring finishes. Reine Wisell had fulfilled his contracted BRM race quota and was looking for a couple of races to showcase his talents for 1973. His reappearance at Lotus was triggered by Dave Walker's suspension by team manager Peter Warr after the Australian had tested a GRD F2 car. The Swede retired with a dropped valve, whilst World Champion Fittipaldi finished 11th minus second and third gears, plus a below-par motor.

'Skip' Barber was a successful American driver who won three SCCA championships in the 1960s and back-to-back Formula Ford National Championships in 1969/70. He bought this March 711/5 ostensibly to race in FA (American F5000) but decided to try his hand at GP racing in 1971 as well, non-qualifying at Monaco, starting last and finishing unclassified at Zandvoort, retiring from the Canadian GP, and unclassified again at Watkins Glen because of gearbox failure. In 1972 he used the March in FA and won a race with it, and also entered the Canadian and US GPs. At Mosport he finished last after practice woes, using the same tyres throughout plus a delay to clear a jammed throttle, but fared much better at Watkins Glen, qualifying mid-grid and running well until slowed by fading brakes to finish 16th. The two-year-old March was entered by Gene Mason Racing, and these two races were his final foray in F1. Overall it was a very worthy effort, given his complete lack of experience in anything remotely like a F1 car prior to 1971 and especially as he was 35 years old at the time.

By 1972 Derek Bell was driving the lamentable Tecno PA123 flat 12. He raced it five times this season, posting two DNQs in France and Italy, one DNS in Canada, and two retirements in Germany and here at Watkins Glen where the car was already sick before it started. Tecno was rightly famous for its successful karting, F3, and F2 machines built by the Pederzani brothers of Bologna – Gianfranco and designer Luciano. They attracted backing from Count Gregorio Rossi of Martini & Rossi fame and employed both Bell and Nanni Galli to race these untidy machines with the big radiators they needed to cool the flat-12 motor. Worse was to follow in 1973.

Lotus personnel have always refuted suggestions that Dave Walker received less than equal treatment and inferior engines compared to Emerson Fittipaldi, which Walker claimed. His was a sad experience. The former works Lotus F3 star had a catastrophic F1 career that consisted of 11 starts and no points – seven retirements, three finishes, and one DSQ plus numerous shunts. Michael Oliver writes in *Lotus 72: Formula One Icon* that Fittipaldi spent much time during first practice at the Glen driving both R7 and R5, which left Walker with no car as Wisell was using R6. Eventually the team assigned R5 to the Brazilian, leaving Walker little time to sort out R7 on a track unknown to him. The other two sessions were wet, so Walker ended up on the penultimate row and then retired in the race with engine failure because of an oil leak. It was his final GP start. Wisell, meanwhile, reckons that he had been held in the pits during practice because, in his opinion, 'I was quicker than Fittipaldi at that time – very frustrating!' The Swede finished tenth, whilst Emerson who had been given an experimental compound by Firestone suffered numerous tyre failures, which dropped the car so far behind that it was retired.

→ Phil Kerr recalls in his book *To Finish First* that he offered Jody Scheckter an F2 contract and some F1 testing without consulting fellow directors Teddy Meyer and Tyler Alexander. This caused considerable consternation in the ranks, but Kerr was looking ahead as Hulme was now 36 and Revson 33, and McLaren needed some young blood for the future. Scheckter's extreme speed was without question, although his all-or-nothing style would cause some problems. At Watkins Glen he practised eighth fastest, ran fourth for a time in the McLaren M19A/1 before a spin caused by a shower sent him off track where he was lightly hit by Hill's Brabham. According to *Motor Sport*'s report, the McLaren stalled and refused to fire up, so Jody was given a push start by the marshals. It was only two years since his first FF race and after only one afternoon at Silverstone in a Formula 1 car.

↘ Amongst the autumn-tinged trees of the Finger Lake region Brian Redman races the final Tony Southgate BRM, the P180 with its unique exposed steering wheel, ahead of Amon's misbehaving Matra MS120D in his last drive for the team who were withdrawing from F1. Two P180s were built and this is the original P180/01. Tony Southgate and team-manager Tim Parnell were unable to cope with Louis Stanley's multi-car entries and drivers during the year, and at Watkins Glen the ageing V12 motors were down on power compared to 1971. The drivers were told to use fewer revs to try to lengthen their lifespan, leading Redman to comment that the engine 'wouldn't pull the skin off a rice pudding'. All four retired with assorted engine failures/problems. The last GP of the year ended with a Tyrrell 1/2 led by Jackie Stewart (ahead of Cevert), which must have made Ken wonder what might have been had Stewart been fully fit. Hulme was third, Peterson fourth, and the Ferraris of Ickx and Andretti fifth and sixth. It should be noted that existing Firestone users were the victims of the tyre company's premature retirement announcement, subsequently rescinded, which had affected company morale, and Goodyear had gained a developmental edge.

1973

A HIGH PRICE TO PAY

Two more drivers perished during the 1973 F1 season. Roger Williamson died at Zandvoort and François Cevert at Watkins Glen in horrible accidents that the barriers arguably contributed to. Tyrrell withdrew from the US GP and Jackie Stewart announced his retirement, already long-since decided. It was Stewart versus Fittipaldi and Lotus new boy Ronnie Peterson, which the Scot won, although Lotus took the Constructors' title. Despite early season unreliability Ronnie won four GPs to Fittipaldi's three although the Brazilian just pipped him to runner up position in the World Championship. The remaining three GPs were won by the McLarens of Hulme (one) and Revson (two) and their newcomer Jody Scheckter made quite an impact, literally. James Hunt completed an impressive F1 debut year by finishing fourth at Silverstone, third at Zandvoort and ending the season with second place at Watkins Glen for Hesketh. Ferrari floundered and Jacky Ickx departed, returning only for a one-off drive in a new car at Monza. Brabham and Carlos Reutemann were fast although dogged by unreliability whilst BRM showed brief promise courtesy of ex-Ferrari racer Regazzoni and Niki Lauda, but it was not sustainable. The UOP Shadow team made its debut with Jackie Oliver and George Follmer scoring two third places between them and a sixth for Follmer and also provided a 'customer car' for Graham Hill. Frank Williams seemingly employed every other F1 driver on the planet to no great effect. Goodyear-shod cars won every World Championship round as Firestone had lost their best teams.

⬇ The Hesketh March was the only fully competitive 731 in 1973, thanks to development by Dr Harvey Postlethwaite (aka 'Harvey'), seen here with hand on hip, and the speed of James Wallis Hunt. Pushing his own car is Lord Alexander Fermor-Hesketh, as James strolls alongside to his grid slot on the fifth row at the British GP, Silverstone. Eagle-eyed readers will spot his cut-off boots and exposed toes because of Hunt's rather large feet, and others will see that the March has its original air-box, although race shots show the March with a yellow 'works'-style fitting. This was because the original one was damaged in the infamous first-lap accident. Hunt, of course, finished a spectacular fourth and set fastest race lap in 731/3, which earned compliments from Denny Hulme in his *Autosport* column 'Behind the Wheel', 'Some words of praise for James Hunt are definitely in order and he certainly deserved the Siffert award. … One of his Firestones was right down to the canvas at the finish … but I think it was Hunt more than the March that deserved the credit.'

⬆ At Buenos Aires, Lotus, BRM, March, Surtees, and Williams all had new drivers for 1973. One such was Clay Regazzoni (BRM P160C/01, a new car not the old 01) who is leading Cevert (Tyrrell 006) and Emerson Fittipaldi (Lotus 72D/R7) in the early laps of the Argentine GP. Clay had taken pole position with a really fizzing lap in the final session three-tenths clear of Fittipaldi on the short 2.08-mile (3.345km) circuit. Ickx and Stewart were third and fourth fastest, whilst Peterson in his first JPS race was on the third row with François Cevert. 'Reggae' led for 28 laps, by which time he had Cevert, both JPS drivers, and Stewart joining the fray. Alas, the BRM's Firestone rubber was going off and Clay dropped to seventh whilst the others retired with engine problems. A persistent Fittipaldi chased leader Cevert for many laps, and then with ten laps to go out-braked the Tyrrell and went on to win by 4.7sec, with Stewart third, slowed by a blistered tyre.

↗ This was the first ever F1 World Championship Brazilian GP, and instead of legions of FIA and assorted other officials, administrative personnel, etc. in evidence, as per the modern norm, there was a conspicuous military presence complete with armoured vehicles. Denny Hulme in McLaren M19C/1 cruises down the now familiar pit lane entrance followed by Fittipaldi's Lotus 72D/R7 and one of the Tyrrells. In those days Interlagos measured 4.95 miles (7.96km) per lap and Hulme started from the second row and finished an impressive third in the two-year-old design despite a briefly sticking throttle and an inoperative clutch. The M19C was using the rear suspension from the forthcoming M23, which suited the latest Goodyear rear tyres. Over the weekend Denny also found himself being voted the new President of the Grand Prix Drivers Association.

➡ Although out-qualified by his new teammate, Emerson Fittipaldi led from flag to flag in Brazil, whilst Ronnie Peterson was eliminated by a broken wheel centre, which caused a minor crash. Of note was Carlos Pace's initial charge in the Surtees TS14A/03 No. 6, but he quickly fell back when his Firestones went off and he soon retired with rear suspension problems. Jackie Stewart, No. 3 far left, finished second. For those brought up on the clinical conditions of modern F1, the dust, dirt, and general detritus shown here was typical of Interlagos starts at this time.

◤ Advanced Vehicles Systems was started by American Don Nicholls, who produced the extraordinary AVS Mk1 Can-Am car in 1970. His British-based Shadow F1 team sponsored by Universal Oil Products featured ex-BRM designer Tony Southgate and ex-BRM driver Jackie Oliver, together with former racer and March co-founder Alan Rees. This is the DN1/2A at Kyalami with its Mel-Mag wheels and big rear wing. American George Follmer, who had driven the AVS Mk1 in 1970, is in the driving seat. Behind the car is Tony Southgate, and it will finish sixth here, whilst Oliver in DN1/1A, who qualified over a second quicker than F1 novice Follmer, retired with a seized engine. During practice both cars had required chassis strengthening and missed a practice session, and Follmer also suffered a blown engine. Southgate noted in his book *From Drawing Board to Chequered Flag* that, unlike the smooth-running BRM V12, the Cosworth DFV created serious vibrational problems, which required rubber mountings for instruments and the water/oil radiators.

◀ The Gordon Coppuck-designed McLaren M23 made an impressive debut at Kyalami when Denny Hulme snatched pole position from Stewart's Tyrrell, but the Scot had to start from the back of the grid in Cevert's car after crashing his own Tyrrell. Hulme led away, but a collision between Hailwood's Surtees and Regazzoni's BRM left debris on the track and Hulme suffered a puncture. Stewart, meanwhile, raced through the field and took the lead on lap seven, going on to win the race, but afterwards he was accused of overtaking under yellow flags during the three laps it took to sort out the Hailwood/Regazzoni accident. Stewart denied any wrongdoing and was later cleared of the accusations. Peter Revson finished second in the older McLaren M19C ahead of Fittipaldi's JPS Lotus 72, whilst Hulme was delayed by two stops, for a new tyre and a wheel change, and finally finished fifth. BRM's sponsor Marlboro subsequently gave Mike Hailwood their own Prix Rouge et Blanc award for his selfless courage in rescuing Regazzoni from his blazing BRM, and later Mike also received the George Medal.

▲ Henri Pescarolo had raced the Len Bailey-designed Politoys-Cosworth FX3/1 for Frank Williams at its debut in the 1972 British GP at Brands Hatch, but he smashed it up. The rebuilt car was driven by Chris Amon again at Brands in the John Player Challenge Trophy in October. In 1973 the now-modified car was raced by Nanni Galli in the Argentine and Brazilian GPs, then Jackie Pretorious had a ride at Kyalami. Back to Brands Hatch again for the Race of Champions where Tony Trimmer raced the car (now known as the Williams FX3B-3) to fourth place in a race famously won by Peter Gethin's F5000 Chevron, and which featured James Hunt in a borrowed Surtees TS9 finishing third.

◄ Shadow's triumvirate of Alan Rees, Tony Southgate, and Don Nicholls at the Spanish GP, Montjuich Park, where George Follmer finished third from mid-grid. Teammate Jackie Oliver retired, as did Graham Hill in his new customer DN1. The rest of Follmer's season was nondescript but, given that George was an F1 rookie, 39 years old, did not know the circuits, and it was a brand new team with a brand new car, he acquitted himself extremely well. In Spain there was considerable drama after practice when the rear suspension mountings were found to be cracked, and these had to be welded up using a torch despite the proximity of the rubber fuel cell, which could not be removed in time. Draining the fuel, pulling the cell back and filling the gap with wet rags did the trick, but to quote Tony Southgate, 'I remained calm externally so that the welder could do his job properly and not be flustered by me, but inwardly I was shitting myself.'

◄ Ronnie Peterson in the JPS Lotus 72E/R8 and Denny Hulme in the McLaren M23/1 lead away from the field at the start of the Spanish GP. Right at the back is Graham Hill's new 'customer' Shadow DN1 that has every kind of problem and is many seconds off the pace. The race settled with Peterson pulling away from Stewart's Tyrrell, followed by Hulme, Cevert in the other Tyrrell, and Fittipaldi's Lotus. Meanwhile, BRM were suffering overheating Firestones (again). Later in the race Fittipaldi ran over accident debris and thereafter nursed a slow rear-tyre puncture, leaving Peterson to a seemingly certain win until his gearbox broke. Stewart also retired and the Brazilian sympathetically stroked his car home to victory ahead of Cevert's Tyrrell, which was similarly delayed by a puncture. Notwithstanding this it would have been a different result if Reutemann's new Brabham BT42 had not retired.

⬆ Following Jo Siffert's fatal accident in 1971 new regulations concerning fire risk came into force at the 1973 Spanish GP. McLaren, Brabham, Shadow, and Surtees had already produced new 'deformable' cars, whilst Tyrrell, BRM, and Lotus modified existing structures, which left March, Williams, Tecno (DNA), Ensign (DNA) and Ferrari to present their new cars. Mauro Forghieri had been displaced at Ferrari after his new B3 had been disparaged during testing in late 1972, and this is the new B3 drawn by Sandro Colombo and built in England by John Thompson's TC Prototypes. As raced it had a front radiator after a side radiator version was rejected, and both cars taken to Spain were reserved for Ickx, which left Merzario without a drive. Its squared-off aesthetics and large size was in stark contrast to its predecessors, and here Ickx in 312B3/010 leads Mike Beuttler's March 731 (just to confuse us these 731s all had existing 721G chassis plates, in this case 721G/2). Ickx qualified sixth, raced sixth, but ended up 12th after stopping to have his brakes bled, whilst Beuttler qualified at the back but drove well to finish seventh.

The first paragraph of *Motor Sport*'s Belgian GP race report stated, '… and through general mismanagement on the part of all concerned the event must rank as the absolute bottom in the long history of the Belgian GP. … Last year the Grand Prix was revived on the Nivelles-Baulers Autodrome, and it all seemed a bit of a joke as regards being the Belgian GP. This year it moved to Zolder and was such a huge joke that it was no longer funny, it was depressing in the extreme.' These trenchant comments were courtesy of the ever-blunt Denis Sargent Jenkinson. In 1973, negotiations for the running of the Belgian GP were not completed until the eleventh hour, resulting in a hasty resurfacing, which began to break up causing the drivers to threaten rebellion. The Terlaemen corner collected Revson's McLaren M23/2 (lap 34) nearest to camera, Peterson's Lotus 72D/R6 (lap 43), Oliver's Shadow DN1/1A (lap 12), and at the back Hailwood's Surtees TS14/04 on lap 5. Later still, Jarier joined the oops brigade with the works March 731. After the race only Tyrrell had survived with both cars intact and, most importantly, finished 1/2 with Fittipaldi's ailing JPS Lotus 72 third.

Chris Amon had reportedly agreed to rejoin March for 1973, but it was Jean-Pierre Jarier who got the drive, and the former works Ferrari, March, and Matra driver found himself driving for Tecno. The team came to Zolder with its new Martini-sponsored Alan McCall-designed PA123/6 with the flat-12 motor which now had better head gasket sealing. However, New Zealander McCall (ex-McLaren and designer of the F2 Tui) had already left the team after initial testing, having fallen out with Luciano Pederzani. Amon was predictably none too happy about progress and complained to Martini, which resulted in an even more unsatisfactory creation. To his credit he finished an exhausted sixth here, and D.S.J. noted that it was a nice-sounding car but not very interesting to look at, what do you think? As an aside, the Belgian GP saw the introduction of allotted race numbers to each team that lasted the season, which still appertains to this day.

The rise and rise of James Hunt from rapid but crash-prone 'Shunt' during his formative years to F1 in 1973 needs no repetition here, or that of his mentor Lord Alexander Hesketh. In the style that the public came to expect and the press played on, Hesketh, 'Bubbles', Harvey, James, et al. arrived at Monaco with more than just a car, transporter, and supporting team personnel. His Lordship had rented the huge *Southern Breeze* yacht, once owned by industrialist John Bloom, and he also brought this Bell Jet Ranger 2 helicopter. Here, in his immutable words, is D.S.J.'s take on this, '… James Hunt driving a March for the Hesketh Racing team, the car all pure and white and Lord Hesketh's personal property, he being his own sponsor if you feel a team must be sponsored these days. …' Hunt qualified on row nine and was running sixth when the March's engine blew up near the end, and he was classified ninth.

In 1973, Monaco's curving run from Tabac to the Gasworks hairpin was irrevocably altered, the roadway now accommodating a 'chicane' leading into a short straight, ending in another left/right and continuing on to curve left into the right-hander La Rascasse, a sharp right around a restaurant, and then a quick squirt before turning right again where the former hairpin had been. Gone were the exposed roadside 'pits', these now being safely tucked away between the harbourside road and the start/finish straight. This is 1960s Cobra and Chevron racer David Purley, who moved to F3 in 1970, being noted for his fearless driving and a hat trick of wins on the daunting Chimay circuit in Belgium. He moved up to F2 in 1972, although in 1973 had dropped back to Formula Atlantic combined with hiring this March (originally 721G/1 but now described as 731/1) for GP racing that carries the logo of the family LEC refrigeration company. He made his first GP start at Monaco from the penultimate row with Graham Hill but retired on lap 32 with a split fuel collector tank.

Denny Hulme rounds what was still known as Station Hairpin (although the station was long gone) in the McLaren M23/1 at the 31st Monaco GP on 3 June 1973. The ever-competitive Denny was third fastest, with Stewart on pole from Peterson's Lotus, whilst Cevert and Fittipaldi (E.) lined up fourth and fifth respectively. Alas, Hulme was delayed by a loose gear lever, which cost him two laps, but he did finish sixth in a race won by Stewart just ahead of Fittipaldi's JPS Lotus (these two collided on their slowing-down lap) whilst teammate Peterson, his car slowed by a lack of fuel pressure, was third, but only thanks to retirements. Standing directly in front of the palm tree and in line with the McLaren cockpit in yellow shirt and striped trousers is legendary F1 photographer Rainer Schlegelmilch.

⬆ By 1973 Reine Wisell's tenure in F1 had become transient. He had only two GP entries in 1973, one here at Sweden with this lurid yellow March that is David Purley's Monaco car 731/1. Pierre Robert was an aftershave product. The car broke its left front suspension during the warm-up lap and did not start. Meanwhile, Ronnie Peterson occupied pole position again, but the delayed race (caused by safety concerns over the number of photographers on the grid/edge of track) was another let down for the Swede. For most of the race Peterson and Fittipaldi were welded together, but then Emerson's car developed braking problems caused by a gearbox oil leak, and he retired with four laps to go. The malevolent fate that dogged Peterson at Lotus then struck again as a left rear tyre puncture slowed him, but he fended off Stewart who suddenly slowed with fading brakes. However, nothing could prevent Hulme from passing him to win the race, and once again Peterson was denied his deserved victory, most cruelly too, given that this was the Swedish GP. Not a good day for Swedish F1 drivers then.

→ Some PR grandstanding here in the Paul Ricard pits. From left to right we have Scheckter and Hulme with Denny's M23/1, Merzario and Ferrari 312B3/012, Emmerson Fittipaldi and Lotus 72E/R5, Wilson Fittipaldi and Brabham BT42-4, Jarier and March 731/4, Tyrrell 006/2 without Stewart, and Graham Hill (for once not giving a two-fingered salute) in his Embassy Racing Shadow DN1/3A. Centre stage is Jackie Oliver's Shadow DN1/4A with him sitting on the rear tyre, and George Follmer holding the top of the air-box. The UOP Shadows had new but incorrectly manufactured rear spring brackets, which caused problems, but even so they were puzzled to be out-qualified by Hill's 'customer' car. Indeed this was Graham's best showing with the Shadow during 1973. He ultimately finished tenth after a recurrence of a practice malady following a competitive mid-field race.

→ Morris Nunn had been a successful and rapid F3 racer and constructor during 1965–72 and one of his drivers, American-born Rikki von Opel, won the 1972 Lombard North British F3 Championship. Liechtensteiner von Opel, great-grandson of Opel founder Adam Opel, commissioned 'Mo' to build a F1 car, and it finally appeared at Paul Ricard for the French GP. It had an aluminium monocoque clad in a Specialised Mouldings glass-fibre body with very individual features and styling. Doug Nye notes in his *History of the Grand Prix Car 1966–85* that Peter Gethin had assisted during initial testing. Von Opel qualified it last but within the 10% cut-off rule, and finished 15th and last, achieving at least some symmetry for the new F1 constructor/team/car/driver.

⬆ *L'Équipe* editor to his ace 'snapper' Jean: 'Now listen I want a really great picture of the winner crossing the line at Paul Ricard.' Jean shrugs and barely disturbs the fat, pale yellow, untipped Boyard between his lips as he mutters, 'Mais, oui.' Ronnie Peterson finally wins a World Championship race, although it was Jody Scheckter who led for 41 laps whilst the Swede chased him for 21 laps before letting Fittipaldi through to see if he could pass the South African. The Lotus 72s were quicker through the bendy bits, but the McLarens had more straight-line speed. However, on lap 42 Jody and Emerson collided whilst lapping a backmarker, and both had to retire. Ronnie takes the flag from the light blue suit in the JPS 72E/R6, the 72s' rear wings now sited 10in further back, whilst our intrepid lensman takes what one hopes was the shot of a lifetime. Cevert finished second for Tyrrell, and Carlos Reutemann scored Brabham's first podium finish in two years with third place. In the background is Fittipaldi's abandoned 72E/R5 with its broken front suspension.

↗ The 5 July 1973 *Autosport* Pit and Paddock opening piece was headed 'Amon and Tecno discord'. It described how Amon and team-manager David Yorke had arrived at Paul Ricard expecting to see the new Tecno Goral E731, but in fact the car was still in Bologna. Amon had persuaded Martini to contact Gordon Fowell and Alan Phillips of Goral consultancy to design the car, which was another built by John Thompson of TC Prototypes. Apparently Tecno wanted more money and Amon rued the fact that he was contracted to Martini rather than Tecno, which prevented him from driving for another team. As can be seen, this was a very different sort of car, visually at least, and reminds us of how much more variation was possible design-wise in those far-off days. The car had a tired engine and Amon did only two single laps because of a seating problem, and then the oil catch tank began filling up. Instead he raced the McCall chassis, starting last, and completed all of seven laps before stopping with no fuel pressure.

➡ Tom Wheatcroft's doomed protégé, the brilliant Roger Williamson, qualified the works/Wheatcroft 731/4 towards the back of the grid because of a brake problem, and then sadly his was one of nine cars (out of 28 starters) that were unable to restart the British GP following the Scheckter incident. It was his first F1 race, and tragically far worse was to follow. Note the decal in the side pod that reads WHEATCROFT Developer.

← Motor Racing Developments had struggled through 1971/72, but fortunately they had employed Gordon Murray during 1970 in the drawing office. South African-born Murray had contemplated leaving at the end of 1971 but ultimately stayed on, although he was approached in late 1972 by Tecno who wanted a new chassis for their flat-12 motor. When designer Ralph Bellamy moved to Lotus, Bernie Ecclestone offered him Bellamy's job and he produced the BT42 type seen here. The first car was raced by the team's F2 driver John Watson in the Brands Hatch Race of Champions but 'Wattie' crashed because of a jammed throttle, breaking his leg and wrecking the car. Two new BT42s appeared in Spain, and at the Swedish GP Reutemann finished fourth, followed up by third in France, as already noted. This is BT42/3, Reutemann up, displaying its separated front radiators (à la BT34), distinctive pyramid shape, and narrow, compact dimensions, as Murray walks away. Carlos qualified on the third row and finished sixth, concerned that his experimental rear wing had cost him straight-line speed.

← Mike Hailwood, Surtees TS14A/04, occupied the middle of the fourth row at Silverstone, but both he and Carlos Pace were eliminated from the GP in the infamous Jody Scheckter crash and were unable to take the restart. Subsequently John Surtees blamed Jody for the carnage, but there were other factors involved. In the first start Lauda's BRM snapped a half-shaft and was hit by Oliver's Shadow, and as the DN1 limped away the marshals pushed the BRM off the grid. In the 19 July 1973 *Autosport* a letter was published from spectators Edward Fitzgerald and David L. Byers of Dublin stating that there was a pool of oil on the grid which went unnoticed in the scramble to remove Niki's car, dropped by somebody with a leaking catch tank on the warm-up lap, and it was Jody's assertion that he had hit some oil which caused him to lose control. The restarted race was ultimately won by Peter Revson (who had placed a £100 bet on himself to win), having overtaken Ronnie Peterson during a brief period of light rain, with a closing Denny Hulme third, whilst Stewart had spun off on lap seven, and Fittipaldi retired with a failed CV joint.

⬆ Including the British GP, Frank Williams had run Ganley, Galli, Pretorius, Belso (DNS in Sweden), Pescarolo, and now Graham McRae at Silverstone. Later came van Lennep, Schenken, and finally Ickx at Watkins Glen. The rapid New Zealander McRae is best remembered for his F5000 prowess, winning the 1972 L&M series in a Leda, and Silverstone was his only GP start. 'Cassius' was not exactly pleased with his ill-handling and troublesome car (chassis 01 that had been refitted with an earlier wide track configuration) and he qualified on the penultimate row. His opinion of the car plummeted further when he had to retire on lap one with a sticking throttle. Behind McRae in the pit lane is Jackie Stewart with the side-radiator/chisel-nose version of 005 that made several practice appearances during 1973.

Zandvoort was notable for its pits roof being an observation platform for lap scorers and observers, and Bette Hill looks down on her husband's Shadow DN1/3A during practice. His permanent leg injuries and anno domini aside, Graham Hill's 1973 form was undoubtedly compromised by the Shadow and he had a dreadful year with it, the French GP being his best showing in race pace terms. Amidst the sand dunes of the Dutch coast Graham's car featured bodywork changes to improve cooling, and he completed practice without any mechanical failures. However, he was still far down the grid, albeit faster than Follmer's works Shadow. Hill was running ninth but ultimately finished unclassified having to stop every few laps to take on water – presumably the engine block had cracked. Beyond the Shadow and standing just inside the white line wearing a black jacket is the car's designer, Tony Southgate.

Autosport's editorial of 2 August 1973 concerning the Dutch GP stated that 'Anybody who saw the television film of Roger Williamson's accident at Zandvoort last Sunday, whether he is a motor racing enthusiast or not, will have been shocked, horrified and disgusted.' David Purley's heroic attempt to save Williamson (for which he was awarded the George Medal) whilst others stood around, was a damning indictment of official incompetence. The circuit had new Armco barriers, but the posts were reportedly only sunk into the sandy soil and the Armco folded over launching the March. Critical remarks in Paddy McNally's Autosport column of 9 August 1973 about Max Mosley's discussions to an informal group of journalists about the accident resulted in a stinging riposte in the magazine's correspondence pages of 23 August. Mr Mosley ended by observing that, 'When one is doing one's best to clarify the little evidence available it is irritating, to say the least, to be accused of being unwise and unconvincing by some dreary gossip writer like McNally.' The distress of Jackie Stewart, François Cevert, and Bernard Cahier is all too apparent after the race in which the Tyrrell drivers finished first and second ahead of an ever-improving James Hunt.

→ The poor performance of Colombo's Ferrari B3, dissatisfied drivers, and finally the intervention of Fiat who were paying for the pleasure, resulted in Mauro Forghieri being reinstated as engineering head of Maranello's F1 team. Furthermore, Ickx's 20th-place grid position at Silverstone had led Enzo Ferrari to withdraw from the Dutch and German GPs, and later it was mutually agreed to terminate Ickx's Ferrari contract. Thus Jacky attended Zandvoort as a spectator, where he had talks with McLaren, who agreed to let him use the spare M23/4 at the Nürburgring, seen here in the pits with Phil Kerr (left) and Teddy Meyer in attendance. It was a one-off drive and Ickx qualified fourth despite an engine failure, and he finished third behind another Stewart/Cevert Tyrrell 1/2, which was to be Stewart's fifth win of the season and his 27th and final GP victory.

→ Hesketh had missed the German GP in deference to development testing, and turned up in Austria with their March wearing a different nose with a pronounced bottom lip, a smaller, more forward-mounted rear wing, and other aerodynamic changes. During pre-race running on the Wednesday an incorrectly sized rear wheel caused a total deflation of a tyre at very high speed, but fortunately only minor damage from a slight impact. Despite the car's improved top speed, Hunt was no quicker pro rata than he had been elsewhere, and qualified ninth but retired with a broken fuel metering unit only four laps into the race. The shot-blasted forward surfaces are perhaps the result of the aforementioned 'off', whilst somebody has mischievously christened the car's new visage 'SILLY NOSE'.

⬆ Ferrari's infrequent withdrawals from F1 over the decades never lasted long, and so it was at the Österreichring for the Austrian GP. Arturo Merzario was the sole driver in the now radically changed B3/011 that, although still based on the Thompson monocoque, featured new bodywork, resited radiators and oil tank, altered suspension geometry, and more, courtesy of Mauro Forghieri. 'Little Art' qualified sixth fastest and raced in fourth place for a few laps, but after a collision with Cevert, which eliminated the Tyrrell, the Ferrari dropped back and finished seventh. This performance apparently tempted Ickx back into the team for Monza, but it was another one-off and the Belgian finished eighth. The race was won by Ronnie Peterson, who let Emerson by so that the Brazilian could win the race and close the championship gap to Jackie Stewart. Alas, a pipe feeding the fuel-metering unit pulled off and Fittipaldi was out only six laps from the end.

⬅ Wilson Fittipaldi in the Brabham BT42/2 with its raised front 'winglet' at the Österreichring. Whilst Reutemann qualified competitively in the No. 1 car, Fittipaldi and Stommelen were slowed by fuel problems and were languishing towards the rear of the grid. This was repeated in the race, with Reutemann finishing fourth and the other two retiring, Wilson with a faulty fuel metering unit, which seems to have been a persistent problem for many at the time. The elder brother could never hope to match his brilliant sibling and he left Brabham after two seasons to develop the Copersucar project, which made its race debut in 1975, of which more anon.

Niki Lauda had shown his true potential at BRM during the year despite the car's frailties, and his impressive German GP qualifying lap, only 2.1sec slower than Stewart's pole time, was significant. At Monza Niki had a new chassis (P160E-10) but he started from the eighth row 2.46sec off Peterson's pole time (the Swede's seventh in 1973) and then had a high-speed crash at the Parabolica on lap 33, fortunately without injury. The BRMs had struggled in 1972 on power circuits, and despite improvements their aged V12 motor was still inadequate. Lauda is followed by Graham Hill's even slower Embassy Racing Shadow DN1/3A, which finished 14th. Meanwhile, Ronnie Peterson's flag-to-flag victory at the Italian GP just ahead of his teammate guaranteed Jackie Stewart's third F1 title. When it became obvious that the Scot would finish fourth (after being delayed by a deflating tyre) Emerson Fittipaldi's chances of winning the championship were all but gone.

There were three March 731s at Monza – James Hunt in the Hesketh 731/3, Mike Beuttler in the Clarke-Mordaunt-Guthrie-Durlacher 731/2, and David Purley back in the LEC 731/1, which was used in Austria as a works entry for Jarier. March themselves did not enter here. Purley qualified last and finished ninth, whilst Hunt posted a DNS because of a practice crash. Hesketh were in the news elsewhere when *Autosport* and *Motor Sport* reported that former BRM engine-designer Aubrey Woods was going to build the team a V12 motor for the latter half of 1974. Beuttler, seen here, really went well, starting mid-grid and running ninth, but ultimately retired when the gear lever came off. At the end of the season, Mike, who was the brother of the Hon. Alan Clark's wife Jane, retired from racing and eventually his lifestyle caught up with him and he died of AIDS-related complications on 29 December 1988 in San Francisco.

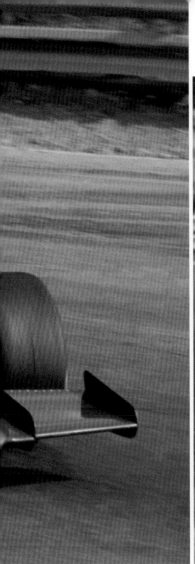

⬉ The Canadian GP at Mosport Park provided drama when BRM sacked Clay Regazzoni, without informing Marlboro, after he had criticised the team's management and cars. Additionally he claimed not to have been paid since the Argentine GP and wondered if the cheque he was subsequently given would be honoured. He was replaced by former team-driver Peter Gethin. Clay was heading back to Ferrari, joining fellow BRMer Niki Lauda, whilst Merzario was departing Maranello. Meantime, Chris Amon was finished with Tecno, having failed to qualify either car in Austria and in Canada. He was driving the third Tyrrell, Depailler having injured himself riding a motorcycle. Chris raced 005 in wedge-nose and side-radiator form, it having only been used like this during practice until now, and he finished tenth in the confusing race, having started on the sixth row.

⬅ The Canadian GP was a chaotic race with changing conditions, many pit stops and tyre changes and confusion about who finished where and why. It seems certain that Peter Revson in the McLaren M23/2 finally won the race that had been led by Lauda's BRM and briefly Fittipaldi, but Jackie Oliver told the author in late 2011 that he was not wholly convinced that Emerson Fittipaldi had actually finished second, whilst Jackie was credited with third place in the Shadow DN1/6A. Revson (right) and Oliver (left) are followed by the works March 731/1 of Jarier, arm raised and about to pit, who finished unclassified, and Tim Schenken in Williams Iso-Marlboro IR/01, who came home 14th. It was Revson's second and final GP win.

⬆ The final race of a fraught and tragic year provided Ronnie Peterson with his fourth GP victory in the Lotus 72E/R6, albeit less than a second ahead of James Hunt in the Hesketh March 731/3 at the end. Despite winning four GPs to Fittipaldi's three, Ronnie's early season woes dropped him to third place in the World Championship, the Brazilian finishing sixth here for his final Lotus outing and still suffering pain from his Zandvoort ankle injuries. Carlos Reutemann achieved another third for Bernie, with Hulme fourth and Revson fifth in his final GP with McLaren. There had been open comment during the latter half of the season about Jackie Stewart retiring and who might replace him at Tyrrell. In fact, François Cevert had been chosen as their new numero uno, but his fatal practice accident changed everything. The team, which included Amon again, withdrew from the GP and thus Stewart non-started in what would have been his 100th and final GP.

1974

NEARLY A CHANGE IN THE STATUS QUO

Emerson Fittipaldi's move to McLaren for 1974 was blessed with three GP victories and a World Championship. Brabham, Ferrari, JPS Lotus and Tyrrell also won races in a season of surplus teams and drivers. Cosworth DFV powered cars won 12 of the 15 GPs. Under the reinstated Mauro Forghieri, Ferrari won three GPs, two for the newly employed Niki Lauda and one for a returning Clay Regazzoni, who finished as championship runner-up. The Swiss might have won it if Ferrari had not let him down badly at the last race. It was Denny Hulme's final year in racing and he duly won the opening race in the Argentine but the rest of his season with McLaren was a write-off. They also fielded a Yardley car for Mike Hailwood but this arrangement was ended by Hailwood's German GP accident. Tyrrell employed Jody Scheckter and Patrick Depailler, Scheckter winning two GPs with eight consecutive finishes. Brabham achieved three victories with Carlos Reutemann but the cars were otherwise still unreliable. Lotus persevered with the new 76 but it was a disaster for Peterson and new signing Jacky Ickx and the team's three GP wins were all courtesy of Peterson in the updated 72. Surtees endured a truly awful year with Pace and Mass leaving for Brabham and McLaren respectively and then suffering Koinigg's fatal crash at Watkins Glen. Shadow meanwhile lost their new signing Peter Revson at pre-race testing at Kyalami when the American became another victim of the Armco barrier. They also ran Jean-Pierre Jarier and later Tom Pryce. More regulatory changes diminished the efficiency of the rear wings and tyres were wider still.

The gap at Shadow left by Peter Revson's death was briefly filled by motor racing polymath Brian Redman, who complained that the Shadow DN3/3A understeered unless he really hurled it into corners – as demonstrated here in the Spanish GP at Jarama. Brian finished seventh, whilst a following John Watson in the John Goldie Racing with Hexagon of Highgate Brabham BT42-2 came home 11th. The third car is Hans Stuck's works March 741/1 (the team were now employing Hans and Vittorio Brambilla) and the German was to finish a meritorious fourth, his best GP result of 1974.

↖ Arturo Merzario was one of many drivers who found themselves changing seats for 1974 either by choice or, in this case, *force majeure*. Following the musical chairs driver selection of 1973, Frank Williams began the year at the Argentine GP with one car (the revised John Clarke-designed Iso-Marlboro FW-01, according to stats) for 'Little Art'. It also ran with a different nose and raised full-width front wing. Merzario qualified mid-grid but blew up two Cosworth DFVs over the weekend, retiring on lap 20 on the revised, longer circuit. A typically alert Frank looks around whilst the diminutive Merzario seems barely big enough for the cockpit.

↙ For 1974, Gordon Murray produced the Brabham BT44, an evolved BT42, and two new cars turned up for the Argentine GP. They were driven by Carlos Reutemann and Richard Robarts, sometime FF racer and joint Lombard F3 champion with Tony Brise. He was essentially a rent-a-driver and survived for three races, the last being at Kyalami. His distinguished teammate led the race for many laps before dropping to seventh with a misfire, whilst Robarts in the BT44-2, seen here leading Pescarolo's BRM P160E/10, started near the back and stayed there until retiring on lap 36 with a broken gearbox. One should not judge too harshly as Robarts was too inexperienced for F1 at this point. The GP was won by Denny Hulme, his final GP win, from the resurgent Ferraris of Lauda and Regazzoni, with Mike Hailwood finishing fourth in the Yardley-sponsored McLaren M23 after Peterson and Ickx (JPS Lotus), and new McLaren signing Emerson Fittipaldi, struck trouble.

↑ With Jackie Oliver moving to management, and George Follmer departed, Shadow now employed Peter Revson and Jean-Pierre Jarier. At Buenos Aires the two had collided, but Revson had been very competitive and this continued at the Brazilian GP at Interlagos, where the American was sixth-quickest and raced sixth in the new Shadow DN3/1A. He lasted ten laps in the race before retiring with overheating, something that had first developed during practice. Revson sits in the cockpit of DN3/1A at his final GP, and just under two months later he was fatally injured during pre-race testing at Kyalami when a suspension part failed and the circuit's barriers were set too high for the wedge-shaped noses of contemporary F1 cars. A part of the Revson family who owned the Revlon cosmetics brand, he had first raced in F1 as far back as 1964 with a Lotus 24-BRM. Peter Jeffrey Revson (27 February 1939 – 22 March 1974).

← McLaren acquired not only Emerson Fittipaldi and Mike Hailwood for 1974 but also sponsorship from Marlboro and Texaco, although Mike the Bike's car was still running under Yardley colours. The Marlboro girls are suitably unsubtle in their 'uniform', and those of a certain age will recall this era when ultra-long, flared trousers/jeans with skin-tight waistbands and thighs often concealed platform shoes of such depth (known as 'fitting stools' to the cognoscenti) that the wearer's height remained uncertain until they disrobed. The McLaren on the right with its air-box sitting on the rear wing is probably Fittipaldi's M23/5, and that is surely Denny's M23/6 on the left with his helmet just visible. Beyond is Robart's BT44-2. The race was won by Fittipaldi from Regazzoni's Ferrari, these two having lapped everybody else, with Jacky Ickx third in the JPS Lotus 72.

↑ In a race won by Carlos Reutemann (Brabham BT44), a surprise was the competitiveness of the new BRM P201/01 at Kyalami, designed by Mike Pilbeam, with its fashionable 'pyramid' midriff and mid-mounted radiators just in front of the rear radius arms. Jean-Pierre Beltoise's second-place finish in the nicely presented car was well deserved but a fluke, as well as being the team's last podium finish at this level. Also surprising were the second- and third-fastest qualifying times of Pace (Surtees) and Merzario (Williams), and during the race a ten-car string, including these cars/drivers, contested the places behind Regazzoni's third-placed Ferrari. Other notable entries were the new Lotus 76s for Ronnie Peterson and Jacky Ickx, who collided with one another on the first lap.

⬉ A newcomer to the F1 scene was the Token RJ02, a project begun by Ron Dennis and Neil Trundle of Rondel Racing before the team folded and was taken over by Tony Vlassopulos and Ken Grob (hence Token) and prepared by Neil Trundle. Designed by Ray Jessop, it made its maiden appearance at Silverstone for the International Trophy and was driven by the extraordinarily rapid Tom Pryce. However, it was still not race ready, and practice was spent trying to make it so. Pryce lasted only 16 laps before the car's gearbox failed. Note its V-shaped radiator intake and riveted cockpit panels. Subsequently Pryce started 20th in the Belgian GP before crashing, and then Monaco refused it entry, so the brilliant Welshman drove a March 743 for Ippokampos Racing in the F3 support race and won easily. Following 1974 it was owned by John Thorpe's Safir Engineering company (Range Rover conversions), who entered it at Brands Hatch and Silverstone as a Safir in 1975 for Tony Trimmer, where it finished last – which was the end of its brief racing history.

⬅ The winter oil crisis had delayed the South African GP until 30 March, so there was a frantic rush for British F1 teams to return to England for the BRDC International Trophy at Silverstone on 7 April. The entry included Chris Amon's new Amon AF1 which non-started, plus a varied selection of F5000 machinery. James Hunt was on pole in the Hesketh 308/01, first seen at the Race of Champions, from Ronnie Peterson in the Lotus 76/1, the replacement for the 72. At the start the Hesketh's clutch began to slip and Hunt had to wait for it to cool off, losing many places. Thereafter, as Peterson took the lead from Mass's Surtees, James scythed his way through the field passing the Lotus (which was suffering from overheating rear tyres) on lap 28. Eventually the 76's engine seized, but Hunt was unbeatable anyway and won effortlessly from Jochen Mass. Hunt closes in on Peterson before administering the coup de grâce, and look at the width of those rear tyres.

⬆ The Spanish GP returned to Jarama for 1974 and produced Ferrari's first GP win since Ickx at the 1972 German GP. Niki Lauda just out-qualified Peterson's improved Lotus 76 by 0.03sec, and although Ronnie led the first 20 laps both he and Ickx retired shortly afterwards following tyre changes from wet to dry rubber, leaving Clay Regazzoni to make it a Maranello 1/2 from Fittipaldi's McLaren M23. Meanwhile, Merzario was impressing again in the Iso Marlboro (aka Williams FW03) in fourth place until the car suddenly went out of control and struck the Armco, which bent backwards (Zandvoort 1973?), launching the car over the barrier with the results seen here. A number of people were struck, all supposedly photographers, but amazingly nobody was seriously injured, and even the man pinned under the front of Merzario's car, Italian photographer Giancarlo Piccinnini, was later seen walking around.

⬆ For 1974 the Belgian GP was back at Nivelles-Baulers for 65 laps of the 2.314-mile (3.724km) circuit near Brussels. This is Vern Schuppan in the lurid-coloured Ensign N174/MN-02, Rikki von Opel having left to replace Richard Robarts at Brabham. The operation was now being financed by 'Teddy' Yip, Hong Kong and Macau-based businessman who employed Schuppan. Vern finished three laps down and 15th after fuel feed problems, which was the car's best showing that year. The rest of the card showed one retirement, one retirement/DSQ, one DSQ (for starting unofficially in Sweden) and two DNQs, the sorry tale terminating at the Nürburgring. Thankfully Ensign would return. The GP was won by Emerson Fittipaldi who beat Niki Lauda by the proverbial gnat's whisker, with Jody Scheckter third in the new Tyrrell 007.

⬅ The Lotus 76 or JPS/9 (because it had followed on from the JPS 72/08) was designed by Ralph Bellamy, who had been told by Colin Chapman to produce a car 100lb (45.36kg) lighter than the 72. It featured a hydraulically operated clutch actuated by a gearlever-knob-mounted button, and there was a throttle pedal, two brake pedals in a conjoined V-configuration which allowed right-foot or left-foot braking, and a clutch pedal for starts. Two 76s were built, the first 76/1 (JPS/9) mainly used by Peterson and the second car (76/2 (JPS/10), normally driven by Ickx. They were frequently run during practice but not often raced, although Peterson finished fourth in Germany with 76/2, albeit fitted with the rear end of 72/8. Here is Ickx in the pits at Nivelles with the troublesome car (76/2) which retired because of overheating.

Guy Edwards reached F1 via sports cars and F5000, but his sojourn with Graham Hill was not a happy experience. The first four races of the season produced two finishes (11th and 12th), one retirement, and one DNQ. However, at Monaco he finished eighth and then at Sweden he came in seventh not too far behind his frustrated team leader. Thereafter it was all downhill and a wrist injury caused him to miss the British GP; said injury further compromised him at the Nürburgring where he failed to qualify and he was replaced by Rolf Stommelen. At least the sun was shining in Monte Carlo.

Jean-Pierre Jarier had been running in the top four at Monaco from the start, and briefly occupied second place until Peterson re-passed him on lap 25. The Frenchman in the Shadow DN3/3A settled into third place, which is where he stayed to the end. In a GP career stretching from Monza 1971 (he did not race F1 in 1972) to Kyalami 1983 the talented Jarier surprisingly only scored two more podium finishes, again third places, at Kyalami and Silverstone in 1979. The other Shadow, driven by Brian Redman, was one of the first-lap casualties of the Hulme/Beltoise intimacy, but he had already decided to leave F1. He told *Autosport*, 'There was no problem, the team was fine. It's just that I don't like the hassle and general struggle of Grand Prix Racing.' Ronnie Peterson, back in the Lotus 72E/R8 (the new 76 still proving troublesome), won the race despite collisions with Jarier and Reutemann en route from Jody Scheckter's Tyrrell after the Ferraris failed.

By the time of the Swedish GP a simmering problem had finally erupted. F1 had become very commercially attractive, and some race organisers had begun to think in terms of accepting some (new) entries and refusing others. This would not affect the top teams but everybody else was vulnerable, although the status quo was ultimately maintained with the regulars more or less guaranteed grid space. Here we see Max Mosley attending Reine Wisell in his final GP start (replacing Hans Stuck who was racing a works F2 March at Hockenheim) in the March 741/1. He outpaced teammate Brambilla during practice, but they were way down the order. Wisell retired on lap 59 with suspension failure, whilst Brambilla lost sixth place two laps from the end because of an oil leak. The race was dominated by Scheckter and Depailler in the Tyrrell 007s, followed by Hunt's Hesketh.

This shot of Graham Hill (Lola T370/HU2) cruising past the rough-and-ready pits at Anderstorp might have come from an earlier era but for the 1970s GP cars in shot. For 1974, Hill had taken up with Eric Broadley, who built the Lolas for the twice-World Champion. It was a vast improvement over the Shadow DN1, but neither car nor driver was capable of hitting the high spots any more in F1. Nevertheless, Hill scored six top-ten finishes during a very competitive season, with only three retirements. Sweden was the high point, where he finished sixth. As was his wont, he constantly fiddled with the cars, but he finally admitted that 'the more we experiment the more we come back to Lola's original design!'

When Richard Robarts failed to appear for Brabham at Jarama, *Autosport* asked Bernie Ecclestone if he had been sacked or whether a performance-based exclusion clause had been invoked. A straightforward Bernie replied, 'It has nothing to do with Richard or his performances, it is entirely a question of money. He had a friend, Bruce Giddy, who said he would get the sponsorship or guarantee the amount himself. So far the sponsorship has not been forthcoming and we cannot afford to run Richard in the car. …' His replacement, Rikki von Opel, retired in Spain and Belgium, DNQ at Monaco, finished ninth in Sweden and Zandvoort (seen here) in the Brabham BT44-2 and then posted another DNQ in France, after which he retired from racing. His place was later taken by Carlos Pace who had left Surtees, quoting to the press that he had done so 'before somebody got hurt'. The race was a 1/2 triumph for Lauda and Regazzoni in the Ferraris from the McLarens of Fittipaldi and Hailwood.

Somehow you always expected Patrick Depailler to drive like this, and he rarely let you down. His press-on oversteering style really captures the speed and drama as the Frenchman races on to second place in the Swedish GP at Anderstorp behind Scheckter with Tyrrell 007/2. Note Patrick's intense, focused eyes. The latest Ken Gardner-designed Tyrrell 007 finished fifth in its first race at Jarama for Jody Scheckter, and at Nivelles the South African improved on this by claiming third place. Tyrrell had coped well following Stewart's retirement and the loss of Cevert, and there would be future victories, but the team's long and protracted decline had begun. Unlike the short-wheel-base form of previous Tyrrells, the 007 had a 6in (152mm) longer wheelbase, this extra space being found between the cockpit and the engine for extra fuel capacity. Gone too was the bulbous full-width nose.

⬆ Scuderia Finotto was owned by Martino Finotto, a touring and sports car racer, and the team's sole sponsor was Bretscher, a Swiss manufacturer of solarium and sunbed equipment. Finotto bought two Brabham BT42s (chassis 5 and 6) for Silvio Moser in 1974, but Moser was fatally injured in the Monza 1,000km. So BT42/6 was raced by 1973/74 Le Mans-winner Gérard Larrousse at Nivelles, but he retired, and here in the French GP at Dijon, where he failed to qualify, thus ending his F1 career. This car's air-box must surely qualify as one of the tallest ever. BT42/6 was entered for the Austrian and Italian GPs for Helmut Koinigg and Carlo Facetti respectively, but it failed to qualify at both races. As in Belgium, the French GP, with its long and proud history at Reims, Rouen, Clermont Ferrand, Charade, et al. had been downgraded to a 2.044-mile (3.289km) circuit in the middle of nowhere. Niki Lauda's pole time was just 58.79sec, and DSJ in *Motor Sport* headed his race report 'The 7th Grand Prix of France – Minuscule'. Elsewhere he wrote of reaction to the race, 'Was that really the French Grand Prix?… A great occasion? Not really, but it was a nice, clean, tidy little Formula One race. …' Said race was won by Ronnie Peterson, who beat the Ferrari twins headed by Niki Lauda.

▶ The excess of entries continued at the British GP at Brands Hatch, including the Token jointly entered by Team Harper for David Purley, the Maki F101 for Howden Ganley, Jon Nicholson's Pinch-Lyncar, Lella Lombardi in the Allied Polymer Group Brabham BT42, and the Dempster International March 731 for Mike Wilds. Sadly, none of these qualified. This is former McLaren engine builder, now boss of Nicholson-McLaren Engines, New Zealander John Nicholson in the Martin Slater-built Lyncar 006 (named after his wife) sponsored by Pinch Plant Hire – another of the so-called 'kit cars'. Slater had built a Formula Atlantic car that Nicholson raced successfully during 1973/74, winning two titles with it. In 1974 he also raced the F1 car at the Race of Champions (16th), and at the May Silverstone (sixth). It was rolled out again in 1975 with no success and ended its days driven by Emilio de Villota in the British Group 8 series in 1976/77.

▶ 1974 was the final year that BRM bore any resemblance to a serious F1 team, and it was not only employing three French drivers (Beltoise, Pescarolo, and Migault) but also had, unsurprisingly, French sponsorship from Motul. Jean-Pierre and Henri had the P201s, the former running the latest short-stroke motor to no avail, but it was the older P160E/09 of François Migault that was quickest of the trio by over a second. The race, however, was a disaster with Beltoise finishing 12th, Migault 16th, after two pit stops to fix a loose rear wing, and Pescarolo retired. This is the underrated, versatile Migault at Paddock. Born in Le Mans on 4 December 1944, he died on 29 January 2012 after suffering from cancer over a long period.

More sartorial provocation – the JPS girls at Brands Hatch where Jody Scheckter won the British GP after Niki Lauda had led for 69 laps before pitting with a puncture. The Tyrrell 007 had scored points in every race it had contested thus far, and Jody was now just two points behind Championship-leader Emerson Fittipaldi, who finished second here.

Mike Hailwood MBE (2 April 1940 – 23 March 1981) with Phil Kerr, who ran the Yardley McLaren M23 at the Nürburgring. He started from the sixth row in M23/7 after crashing his regular chassis M23/1 in practice. In the race Mike contested fifth place with Peterson and Ickx, but on lap 12 he landed crookedly after Pflanzgarten and hit the barriers head-on, smashing an ankle, shinbone, and also suffering a complex fracture of the knee. His ankle injuries left him with limited foot mobility and he had to retire from racing, although he did return to his first love to win at the Isle of Man in 1978 riding a Ducati. In *To Finish First*, Phil Kerr related that Mike had been suffering from insomnia in 1974 and started taking sleeping pills, gradually increasing the dosage up to three a night. Following the crash, Hailwood realised that at times his reactions were slow and his memory impaired. Earlier on, Fittipaldi's car stalled on the grid and was hit by Hulme's M23, which promptly retired. Denny then rejoined the race in the spare M23 but was disqualified, whilst 'Emmo' suffered a puncture and having pitted for a new tyre retired with a broken gearbox.

→ John Watson's F1 outings in 1974 for John Goldie/Hexagon had started with a Brabham BT42, but in Germany they had a new BT44 (chassis number 4). However, this is the older car, BT42/2, in which Watson practised but then changed to the BT44 for the race, as the new 1974 rules allowed. This proved to be a mistake because the newer car developed front suspension problems on the first lap and was retired. John looks at our photographer as Henri Pescarolo passes by in the BRM P201/03, which finished tenth here. Is that the doyen of British photographers, Geoff Goddard, standing behind the man holding Watson's rear wheel? Also present was Chris Amon's doomed Gordon Fowell-designed AF1 that Chris (suffering from a heavy cold) and Larry Perkins failed to qualify, a scenario repeated at Monza, after which Amon finished the season driving a BRM.

→ It looks like Niki Lauda is receiving a right royal bollocking from Ferrari-designer Mauro Forghieri, whilst a no doubt equally pissed-off team manager, Luca di Montezemolo, looks on. The faces of the inevitable eavesdroppers bear witness to this 'I'd rather be anywhere but here' moment for Niki after he had collided with Scheckter's Tyrrell on the second corner of the first lap, having made a tardy start from pole position. Scheckter, however, survived to finish second and set fastest lap for his eighth consecutive finish in the points, whilst Clay Regazzoni won the race to most people's pleasure.

⬆ The Österreichring was now the fastest circuit on the GP calendar, and the Austrian GP was a decisive victory for Carlos Reutemann, who led the whole way. He qualified second to Niki Lauda, who pursued him closely for 12 laps before gradually fading away and then retiring with probable valve failure. For a while Carlos Pace held second place in the other Brabham before a fuel line circlip failed, so Denny Hulme took second, with James Hunt third in the Hesketh despite a pit stop. Early in the race Reutemann in the BT44-1 leads Lauda in the 312B3/015, Regazzoni's 312B3/014, and the rest.

↗ Famous BMW touring car racer Dieter Quester raced the third Team Surtees entry TS16-05-03 in Austria with backing from Memphis smokes and Iris ceramics. He qualified last, but this was better than teammates Derek Bell and Jean-Pierre Jabouille who did not qualify, whilst Jochen Mass had left Surtees after a strong performance at the Nürburgring ended in retirement, again, and was heading to McLaren. Dieter, who came ninth, is followed by the ever-determined Ian Ashley giving the Token RJ02 (who had made his difficult F1 debut with the car at the Nürburgring) its final GP appearance where it finished running but unclassified.

➡ The Lotus 76s had finished fourth and fifth in Germany, but at Monza Peterson decided not to race 76/1 seen here, instead using 72/R8 again and winning a close race with Emerson Fittipaldi's McLaren. Poor Ickx had no such choice and was left way down the grid in 76/2, but he did rise to ninth place before a throttle linkage problem stopped him, and two more stops later he retired. The Lotus 76 certainly disproved the old adage 'if it looks good then it probably is'. Behind Ronnie and 'Emmo', Jody Scheckter finished third, and Arturo Merzario scored the final GP points of his F1 career in the Iso Marlboro with fourth place. Nevertheless, it should be noted that the Ferraris of Lauda (1–29 laps) and Regazzoni (30–40 laps) led convincingly until both retired, and third-placed Reutemann also dropped out.

⬆ David Hobbs was another man for all seasons, as it were – sports cars, FJ, F2, F1, F5000, Can-Am, IMSA, Indianapolis, endurance racing, et al. and later commentating. He took over the Yardley McLaren seat in Austria where he finished seventh, but at Monza he qualified near the back of the grid. His first GP outing was at Silverstone in 1967 for Bernard White, then in Germany he raced in the F2 class at the German GP, and later drove White's old BRM P261 at Monza. In 1968 he had a one-off outing in one of the Surtees Hondas at Monza, then forward three years and another one-off drive, this time for Roger Penske in a McLaren at Watkins Glen. David races on to finish ninth at Monza in M23/4 in his final GP.

↗ The Canadian GP was notable for the appearance of two major American challengers, this one being the Vel's Parnelli Jones Racing Parnelli VPJ-4 for Mario Andretti. The car was the work of Maurice Philippe, who had penned the Lotus 72, and it was in fact a lighter, superior version of the 72, which was what Colin Chapman had intended the 76 to be. Here, Mario talks to engineer Rory Byrne, with Philippe in the background. This was Mario's return to F1 after two years, and he qualified just past mid-field despite the inevitable teething problems. A promising run saw him home in seventh place one lap down on Emerson Fittipaldi's winning McLaren M23, with Clay Regazzoni second for Ferrari, and Ronnie Peterson third in the Lotus 72. Ferrari, meanwhile, must have been even more annoyed with Lauda here than they had been in Germany, when the Austrian led the race for 67 laps before crashing.

➡ Chris Amon's 1974 campaign was another disaster, having started with his Gordon Fowell-designed Amon AF101 that was withdrawn from the Silverstone International Trophy, retired in the Spanish GP, and also withdrawn at Monaco. It then disappeared until the German GP where it again failed to qualify, an experience repeated at Monza, after which the car was discarded. So he became another of a long line of BRM drivers of this time for the last two races of the season. Here in Canada he qualified 25th in the P201/4, alarmed by its tendency to weave in a straight line, and finished unclassified after many pit stops. Watkins Glen was better, but ninth place was scant reward for somebody of Amon's former status.

There was much confusion at the start of the US GP when Andretti's car was wheeled off the grid with electrical problems, which allowed first reserve Jose Dolhem in the second Surtees to start the race. At the same time Tim Schenken, who was waiting at the back of the grid with Dolhem in a one-time drive in the Lotus 76/1, apparently misinterpreted the officials and joined in. He lasted six laps before being black-flagged. Here is Schenken in 76/1 with Peter Warr in the pit lane for his final outing in F1. The race gave Bernie Ecclestone's team its third GP victory of the year (Carlos Reutemann), with teammate Carlos Pace second and James Hunt finishing third. Catastrophically, Watkins Glen was again the setting for tragedy when Helmut Koinigg was killed after his Surtees left the track, possibly because of tyre failure, passing through the catch fences before striking the barriers, which once again had not been properly secured, allowing the TS16 to slide between the rails decapitating the driver. Dolhem in the other car was immediately withdrawn. For John Surtees it had been a truly terrible year, which ended in the worst possible way.

The 1974 F1 season was one of the most competitive ever in general terms. McLaren won four GPs (Fittipaldi three, Hulme one), Brabham three (all Reutemann), Ferrari three (Lauda two, Regazzoni one), Lotus three (all Peterson), and Tyrrell two (both Scheckter). Emerson Fittipaldi was the latest F1 World Champion, but he only beat Clay Regazzoni by three points (55 to 52), with Scheckter next on 45 points. Apparently the Swiss had an ill-handling car (allegedly faulty shock absorbers) at Watkins Glen, which dropped him to 11th place and nil points, when third or better would have made him the World Champion. Here is Clay at far right standing by his 312B3/011, whilst a rather rotund officer of the Watkins Glen Police Department perhaps displays contempt for this strange device and probably hankers after a proper race car.

1975

A DIFFICULT YEAR

Ferrari could look back in satisfaction at 1975 with six GP victories for Lauda (five) and Regazzoni (one) and the Austrian's World Championship and Constructors' title. It was Maranello's first World Championship title for 11 years. Their new 312T had finally ended the Cosworth powered cars' long reign. However, it was another year of tragedy with the Spanish GP stopped following Stommelen's crash into the crowd, killing four spectators and Mark Donohue fatally injured during warm up for the Austrian GP. Four races were stopped prematurely, the Spanish as noted plus the Monaco, British and Austrian, the first and last of these scoring half points because they were abandoned before minimum distance. Additionally FOCA boycotted the Canadian GP over money matters and it was cancelled. There were wins for Hunt at Zandvoort in the Hesketh and Brambilla's rain-soaked Austrian triumph whilst McLaren won three races, Brabham two and Tyrrell one. It was the latter that surprised everybody by launching their six-wheeled P34 in late September, which caused much comment. Shadow continued with Pryce and Jarier both showing race-winning potential but it never happened. Of note was Graham Hill's new Hill car but Stommelen's Spanish GP accident was a harbinger of later tragedy, which claimed Graham, his brilliant new driver Tony Brise and team members. Times were tight thanks to an energy crisis (sound familiar?) and Firestone had left the building leaving Goodyear as sole tyre supplier.

Former F3, Formula Atlantic, and F5000 racer Alan Jones began his World Championship quest at the 1975 Spanish GP with the Harry Stiller Hesketh 308-1, but this lasted only until the Swedish GP, after which Stiller disbanded the operation and became a tax exile. This really is putting a wheel in the dirt, as Alan finds the limit and beyond at Anderstorp in the Rob Walker-sponsored car in which recalcitrant machine he finished 11th. It is a fact that nobody else came close to Hunt's speed in these apparently difficult cars. Alan was then invited by Graham Hill to join the Embassy Racing Team starting at the Dutch GP, until Rolf Stommelen returned for the Austrian GP.

A new year and new cars but now no Firestone tyres, so everybody was wearing Goodyear rubber. Wilson Fittipaldi's Copersucar FD-01 made its first race appearance at Buenos Aires. Designed by Richard Divila, there were two different engine covers, one with the orthodox air-box and the other, shown here, with an additional intake atop the other. The car had covered some 1,000 miles in testing, a small part of it by Emerson Fittipaldi, but it proved very problematic and only just qualified within the 110% time rule. This was Wilson's first GP since Watkins Glen 1973 and on lap 13 he crashed the Copersucar, which then caught fire and was destroyed. Ho hum!

James Hunt's nascent race-winning potential almost came to fruition in Argentina with the Hesketh 308-3, which was equipped with rubber front springs. Qualifying sixth, he had taken the lead on lap 25, but then a brief off at the final hairpin allowed Emerson Fittipaldi to assume the lead and he won the race by 5.91sec from a frustrated Hunt. Others had starred here, Jean-Pierre Jarier on pole in the new, higher downforce Shadow DN5/1A, but non-started after its crown-wheel and pinion failed on the warm-up lap, whilst Carlos Reutemann led the first 25 laps before a mistake dropped him back to third, which is where he finished.

↑ The other American entry that made its debut at Mosport in 1974 was Roger Penske's Penske PC1 designed by Geoff Ferris, late of Brabham and driven by Mark Donohue, who had been lured back from retirement. Once again this was a Cosworth DFV/Hewland package, which Donohue placed 12th in Canada but retired at Watkins Glen. In 1975 a second PC1 was built with a wider track, new front suspension, rear wing and air-box. It started 16th and finished seventh in the Argentine GP, and at Interlagos car and driver were towards the rear of the grid again, Mark admitting that he'd taken a wrong turn on chassis tuning. In the race, severe handling problems developed and the car was withdrawn by Roger Penske. I bet the man working on the PC1 was really enjoying Donohue's intense scrutiny, whilst in the background is Graham Hill's Lola T370 HU370-2 (finished 12th), and is that Mario Andretti in red T-shirt in conversation with Frank Williams? The car was beautifully engineered but the team's lack of F1 experience and their unfamiliarity with the circuits meant that they were always behind in terms of set-up, which trapped them towards the back of the grid no matter what they tried.

All of BRM's French racers (including Jean-Pierre Beltoise, who was supposed to be joining a new Ligier team but was displaced by Jacques Lafitte, thus ending J.P.'s F1 career) and sponsors had flown the coop at the end of 1974. So another talented racer, Mike Wilds, found himself in another uncompetitive F1 car (having struggled with Ensign during the latter half of 1974), the BRM P201/4. He qualified 5sec off the pace at Buenos Aires and lasted 24 laps before the oil scavenge pump failed, having driven with verve according to Pete Lyons. At the Brazilian GP the BRM was even slower and then retired after 31 laps when the same loose clutch nut problem that had stopped Beltoise at the start of the 1974 Italian GP repeated itself. Here we see Mike wearing his yellow Griffin helmet, a fashionable choice at the time, in the patriotic red, white and blue Stanley BRM. This was his last drive for BRM and almost his last F1 outing.

The Brazilian GP at Interlagos was destined to be Carlos Pace's only GP victory, a poor reward for a brilliant talent. He beat fellow Brazilian Emerson Fittipaldi and Jochen Mass in the McLarens, but only after Jean-Pierre Jarier (Shadow) had led the race from the fifth to the 33rd lap by an ever-increasing margin before retiring. In the background is Ronnie Peterson, still racing the now almost antique but very finely developed Lotus 72E/R8, although for myriad reasons both JPS 72s were off the pace and Ronnie finished 15th, whilst Ickx managed ninth.

There were new cars from Ferrari, March, and Lola and new existing types from Lotus, Tyrrell, and Shadow at Kyalami. Hill, Brambilla, Lauda, Jody Scheckter, and Merzario all crashed, and others spun off over the three practice sessions. The 1975 Brabhams of Pace (BT44B-2), leading, and Reutemann (BT44B-1) recorded almost identical times to occupy the front row. They are followed away by Scheckter (No. 3) and Depailler (No. 4) in the Tyrrell 007s, Lauda's new Ferrari 312T/018, with Peterson (Lotus 72E/R9) ahead of Andretti in the Parnelli VPJ-4, and Vittorio Brambilla's March 751/1 alongside, and the rest. Pace led for two laps, then Scheckter was past and away, and whilst the Brazilian fell back his Argentinian teammate in the other Brabham assumed second place and chased Jody all the way to the flag, with Depailler third in the second Tyrrell and Pace fourth with handling problems.

◄ *Autosport*'s headline for Pete Lyon's report of the 1975 Spanish GP at Montjuich Park was 'Civil War in Spain', a reference to the improperly constructed and damaged barriers, which were unsecured, and a fatal race crash. Many helped bolt up the aged Armco including Ken Tyrrell, Derek Gardner and Max Mosley, whilst all the drivers except Jacky Ickx who was not a member of the GPDA, refused to practice. Emerson Fittipaldi went home whilst brother Wilson and Merzario drove one lap of the race and pulled out. The race was stopped after 29 of the scheduled 75 laps leaving Jochen Mass in the McLaren M23/8, who had overtaken Jacky Ickx (Lotus), to win with Carlos Reutemann third for Brabham. As a result of the abbreviated race distance only half points were awarded. Note the considerable gaps between and under the Armco rails as Mass passes by.

◄ Tony Brise had his maiden GP outing in Spain in the Williams FW04, an evolved version of the Iso-Marlboro cars with a new monocoque courtesy of ex-McLaren engineer Ray Stokoe. Brise started from the ninth row and finished seventh in the shortened race. This was his only outing for Williams and he then moved to Graham Hill's team for the rest of the season.

▶ Rolf Stommelen's Spanish GP came to an abrupt end when the carbon-filament rear wing supports of his leading Hill GH-2 fractured and the wing flew off just past the pits. In the ensuing crash, which involved Pace's closely pursuing Brabham, the Hill hit the barriers. These, in fact, held firm, but the car passed over the top rail and ended up on its side, killing four people. Stommelen suffered broken bones in both legs, two ribs and a wrist. The car actually stood up remarkably well to the massive impact, given that this is nearly 40 years ago, but note the buckled steering wheel and the engine/gearbox, which was almost ripped off the car as it went in backwards. Pace escaped unharmed and Rolf was back in the team for the Austrian GP just under four months later.

▲ Roelef Wunderink followed Rikki von Opel, Vern Schuppan, and Mike Wilds in driving Mo Nunn's series of Ensign F1 cars. This is the 1974 car (N174 MN02) that the Dutchman drove at the Brands Hatch ROC (unclassified), the Silverstone International Trophy (retired), and the Spanish GP (retired). At Monaco he went one better, or rather worse, by not qualifying. Wunderink was a sometime FF and F5000 racer and his Ensign drive was financed by the Dutch HB Bewaking alarm company. Following Monaco he failed to qualify the new MN04 car in Britain, was not classified in the older MN02 in Austria, failed to qualify it in Italy, and then returned to MN04 at Watkins Glen where he retired, after which he too retired from F1. Despite the team's modest finances the cars were always immaculate, as can be seen.

◄ Niki Lauda's 1974 season was boosted by the return of Mauro Forghieri to the Ferrari F1 team. Two GP victories aside, his two race crashes and a puncture whilst leading the British GP probably cost him the World Championship. For 1975, Forghieri introduced the 312T (Transversale), which featured a transverse-mounted gearbox, the intention being to concentrate as much weight as possible within the now longer wheelbase. Having won the Silverstone International Trophy, Lauda then won at Monaco in the 500bhp 312T/023 starting from pole ahead of Tom Pryce's Shadow. The race began in wet conditions and Lauda led for 23 laps before pitting for 'slick' tyres, briefly allowing Ronnie Peterson into first position. However, Lotus were tardy in changing Ronnie's tyres and Lauda won the race by just 2.78sec from Fittipaldi's McLaren, with Pace (Brabham) third, and the delayed Peterson fourth.

▲ It was back to Zolder for the Belgian GP where we see Carlos Reutemann having a parley with Gordon Murray, whilst 'Herbie' Blash looks at the front suspension and Bernie Ecclestone, in 'shades', walks round behind the BT44B-1. Reutemann finished third here, whilst the other Carlos led the first three laps of the race before dropping to eighth. Then Brambilla led for two laps in the works March before Lauda took over and won his second GP in a row. Jody Scheckter finished second and Depailler fourth for Tyrrell, whilst Brambilla retired with fading brakes.

⬆ Following on from the Token experience, Tom Pryce had joined Shadow at the 1974 Dutch GP, where he collided with Hunt's Hesketh – the duo repeating the contact sport at Dijon. Thereafter, his best result was sixth in the German GP, and thus far in 1975 he had only managed a ninth (at Kyalami) and sixth (at Zolder) and a front row at Monaco where he crashed. The spectacular driving style certainly reflected his raw speed and huge potential. At the Swedish GP in Anderstorp he qualified seventh fastest but stopped on the first lap with jammed throttles, thereby losing a lap, and ultimately clutch problems caused him to spin off.

⬅ Frank Williams had two new drivers at Anderstorp, Merzario having departed. They were Ian Scheckter (for here and the Dutch GP) and the perennially underfunded but very determined Damien Magee. The Ulsterman only managed this one GP start in his career and he acquitted himself well given his lack of F1 experience and finished 14th, two laps down in the old Iso chassis FW03, which had been converted back to the side radiator/original nose configuration. Ian Scheckter, meanwhile, retired the newer FW04 on lap 50 when a tyre burst. The race was another Ferrari triumph for Lauda (first) and Regazzoni (third), split by Reutemann's Brabham.

At the Dutch GP it all came together for the Hesketh team, aided by a canny tyre stop, and Hunt won the race, beating the Ferraris and provoking the establishment with their irreverent celebrating. Here are Le Patron, James, 'Bubbles', and Harvey before the race. An extraordinary collection of ex-public schoolboys vulgarly described as 'toffs' – Lord Hesketh (Ampleforth), Hunt (Wellington), Horsley (Dover College), and Postlethwaite (the Royal Masonic School for boys). The last went on to design cars for Walter Wolf, Ferrari, and Tyrrell, and died aged only 55 on 13 April 1999.

Howden Ganley had twice failed to qualify the Maki F101 (the creation of Kenji Mimura) in 1974, the second ending in a nasty accident at the Nürburgring. A much-altered F101C-02 appeared in 1975, supposedly for Dave Walker to drive in the Belgian and Swedish GPs, but it was a no show. However, the car made it to Zandvoort with one engine (which duly failed) and sponsorship from Citizen Watches, but it was still a crude and poorly constructed device. According to Pete Lyons, 'this effort is just not up to scratch'. Hiroshi Fujida, whose family were the largest kimono producers in Japan, was the first Japanese driver to attempt entry into the F1 World Championship, and he tried and failed again at Silverstone, which ended his F1 aspirations. Then Tony Trimmer attempted the impossible at the Nürburgring (and later the Austrian and Italian GPs) to no avail. Nick Brittan in his *Autosport* column 'Private Ear' noted that 'the mechanical reliability of the car is in keeping with its appearance'.

⬉ With the withdrawal of the John Goldie/Hexagon F1 team, John Watson had joined Team Surtees for 1975. Promising second and fourth places in the non-championship races at Brands Hatch and Silverstone were not replicated in the World Championship, and Watson, one of F1's best drivers in period, found his season going into reverse. In the French GP at Paul Ricard his was the only Surtees on the grid. He qualified the TS16-04-05 on the seventh row and finished 13th, one lap adrift. John passes an out of shape Alan Jones in the Hill GH3, who had joined the team at the Dutch GP and finished 16th here. Later after finishing fifth in Germany he departed as Rolf Stommelen was back in action for the Austrian GP. Team mate Tony Brise, already on board since Zolder, finished seventh at Ricard.

⬅ Having twice failed to qualify in 1974 (French GP for Frank Williams and Austrian GP for Surtees) future Renault ace Jean-Pierre Jabouille was successful at Paul Ricard for his GP debut in the Tyrrell 007/5. He finished 12th, the last car to complete the full race distance. Meanwhile, at the prow, Niki Lauda won his fourth GP of 1975 just 1.59sec ahead of Hunt's Hesketh, which was but 0.72sec ahead of Jochen Mass in the McLaren M23. Of note was the departure of Jacky Ickx from Lotus after the race. According to Ralph Bellamy, Jacky never had the ear of Colin Chapman. His race form had been gradually fading and, combined with the ageing 72 and its unsatisfactory replacement plus a series of front brake shaft failures, he decided to quit.

⬆ Vittorio Brambilla's March 751/3 at the British GP had new front and rear suspension, and these appendages behind the rear wheels. They were fairings designed to smooth out the turbulence behind the tyres, which apparently worked both in the wind tunnel and on track, Brambilla reporting a gain of 200rpm on Hangar Straight. Vittorio and March had been enjoying some very competitive qualifying during 1975, and this continued at Silverstone where he started fifth on the grid and finished sixth in a race cut short by a multi-car accident induced by a sudden rain shower.

⬉ The British GP was decided by the order of the cars on the lap preceding the accidents, which left Emerson Fittipaldi, who had not crashed, the winner from those who had – Pace, Scheckter, Hunt, and Donohue (now March 751-mounted, the Penske PC-1 having been discarded). Apart from the controversial race ending, the British GP was notable for Tom Pryce's pole position, Graham Hill's decision to finally retire after 17 years in F1, the inclusion of a new chicane at Woodcote, and the appearance of Shadow's Matra V12-powered DN7/1A seen here on the Club Straight. This car was unsuccessfully raced twice, in Austria and Italy by Jarier, and then discarded.

⬅ Mario Andretti and the Vel's Parnelli VPJ-4/002 in the Nürburgring pits. He qualified 13th and retired in the German GP because of a fuel leak, which summed up his season apart from fourth and fifth places in Sweden and France. The race was characterised by a rash of punctures, a dozen in total for nine cars, the slick tyres of this time being vulnerable to any track debris. One of these 'flats' cost Lauda the race (he eventually finished third having 'officially' broken the seven-minute barrier during practice) and two others caused big accidents for Scheckter and Brise. Mario retired with a fuel leak, whilst Carlos Reutemann won the GP ahead of Jacques Lafitte, who gave Frank Williams his best result in six years.

⬆ Amongst the lower orders at the Nürburgring were GP rookie, German journalist and racer Harald Ertl, in his privately entered Warsteiner Brewery-sponsored Hesketh 308-1, Wilson Fittipaldi in the Copersucar FD-03, and Gijs van Lennep in the HB Ensign N175 MN04. They finished respectively eighth, retired, and sixth. The Copersucar project had been struggling all year long and would continue to do so, and it was to be the elder Fittipaldi's final season in F1.

◤ Having abandoned the Penske PC1, the Penske team acquired a new March 751/5 but the basic problems remained – their unfamiliarity with the circuits and set-up. At the Österreichring during pre-race warm-up Mark Donohue left the track at the Vöst-Hurgel curve (as it was pre-1977) when the left front tyre deflated, the car mowing down several rows of catch fencing, which helped launch it over the barrier. The 751 passed through some plastic advertising banners supported by metal poles, one of which hit Donohue's helmet. There were only a few yards 'twixt track, catch fencing, and the barrier. Initially unconscious, he was brought round by an injection and had no obvious physical injuries but soon developed head pains and was taken to hospital in Graz and operated on to remove a blood clot. He never regained consciousness and died at midnight on 19 August 1975. Two marshals were also injured in the accident, and one, Manfred Schaller, passed away soon after. In the picture Mark is looking at Penske team-manager Heinz Hofer, ex-Swiss national ski team racer who had met Roger Penske during skiing at Vale years before. Sadly, Hofer died in a UK road accident in late December 1977. On the right is crew-chief Viennese Karl Kainhofer, whose association with Roger Penske extended back to the late 1950s.

◄ The Austrian GP was another race in 1975 that only scored half points because positions were decided after 29 of the planned 54 laps due to severe wet weather conditions. Vittorio Brambilla (centre) won deservedly even if he did crash after crossing the line. However, not long afterwards the weather began to clear and there were calls for the race to be restarted, much to March's distress. Enter the ever-aware Mr Mosley and the FIA rule book, wherein it is stated that a race can only be restarted if it had been stopped by a chequered flag 'in conjunction with a black flag', which of course it had not. The 37-year-old Brambilla looks justifiably pleased, whilst third-placed Tom Pryce seems somewhat less than happy with second-placed Mr Hunt. Perhaps he is recalling their two consecutive collisions at the start of the Dutch and French GPs in 1974.

↑ In the best of all Ferrari worlds, the Italian GP at Monza should be won by a Ferrari driven by an Italian driver. Clay Regazzoni was not Italian, but the next best thing, hailing from Mendrisio, near Lugano, in the Ticino, the Italian-speaking region of Switzerland. Clay, in the Ferrari 312T/024, shared the front row with pole sitter Lauda and led the race flag to flag, whilst Niki followed until a rear damper failed, letting a very hard-driving Emerson Fittipaldi take second place with six laps to go. Thus Lauda finished third and became the 1975 F1 World Champion. For a while the Italian GP had been threatened by inclement weather, having rained heavily on and off during Saturday night and Sunday morning. Then, miraculously, the clouds cleared, the sun came out and the track gradually dried, as can be seen here.

◤ Tony Brise was undoubtedly going to be one of the best F1 drivers of the era, but fate was cruel to both him and, later, to Tom Pryce. At Monza, Brise qualified sixth in the Hill GH1-4, his best grid position so far, but he was the victim of the first chicane on the second lap, as indeed were others including teammate Stommelen. At Watkins Glen Tony hit Brian Henton's spinning Lotus on lap six, which tore off the Hill's right rear wheel, and that was it. Brise was one of the five people who died in Graham Hill's Cessna air crash on Arkley golf course on a foggy November night, and what might have been never was. Anthony William Brise, 28 March 1952 – 29 November 1975.

◤ Successful Formula Atlantic racer Jim Crawford had a Lotus testing contract and they ran him in the British GP, where he crashed out. At Monza Crawford was running the now rebuilt Lotus 72E/R5 in unloved long-wheelbase form with wide front track and rear coil springs, which he did not like at all. It suffered excessive understeer and he qualified last but one, and was hit by Stommelen's Hill on the first lap, which punctured a tyre, necessitating a pit stop. The Scot ended up 13th. It was his last GP, and after this he worked for Toyota in Switzerland before returning to Britain in 1979 and the start of several years of British formula racing before emigrating to America in 1982. He successfully competed in Can-Am before joining the Indycar series, but suffered a dreadful crash at Indianapolis in 1987, which smashed his feet and ankles. Having recovered from this he returned to finish sixth in 1988, but since 1986 had only been racing at the Brickyard, and he continued up to 1995, having failed to qualify in 1994/95. He finally retired, moved to St Petersburg, Florida, and became a fishing boat captain before dying of liver disease in Tierra Verde, Florida, aged only 54 years. Jim Crawford, 13 February 1948 – 6 August 2002.

◤ Jochen Mass had joined McLaren for the 1974 Canadian GP, finishing 16th, and he was then seventh at Watkins Glen. During 1975 he had won the foreshortened Spanish GP and enjoyed six points-scoring finishes, including three third places, the last coming at Watkins Glen. This practice shot reveals how vulnerable pit lanes were at the time, with their wide, unprotected entry, as the McLaren personnel tend to Jochen's M23/6. Niki Lauda won the US GP, his fifth win of the season, from Emerson Fittipaldi's McLaren, with Mass third, as noted. 'Emmo' must have been experiencing a sense of déjà vu as he prepared to leave McLaren to join brother Wilson's Copersucar project.

Lotus had also run John Watson (briefly unemployed) at the German GP, and Brian Henton (British, Austrian and US GPs) during 1975, and Brian was only two-tenths slower than Ronnie during a Silverstone test. Henton was classified 16th in the rain-shortened British GP after crashing, non-started at the Österreichring because of a practice accident, and finished 12th at Watkins Glen. The highly talented Henton went on to become a F2 champion, but his F1 career was scuppered by lack of funding and uncompetitive machinery. This was the final GP start for the type 72, which had remained fully competitive until 1975, when the ever-changing and prohibitive regulations, and the evolving tyres, finally overwhelmed the ageing design.

MORE POLITICKING AND
GOODBYE NÜRBURGRING

Lord Alexander Hesketh's brief reign as F1's aristocratic winning team owner was at an end with James Hunt going to McLaren where he ultimately became World Champion beating Niki Lauda by just a single point. The season was marred not only by Lauda's near fatal injuries at the German GP but also by much politicking and controversies with Hunt being disqualified twice, at the Spanish GP where he had finished first and at the British round which he also won. His Spanish win was reinstated but he lost the argument over the British race. Nevertheless despite a massive points deficit after assorted problems Hunt gradually eroded Lauda's lead, undoubtedly helped by Niki's accident. A farcical Italian GP where McLaren and Penske were targeted over alleged fuel irregularities heightened tensions. The six-wheeler Tyrrell scored one victory in Sweden and eight second places between Scheckter and Depailler plus another second for Depailler in the old 007. Single race winners were Regazzoni Ferrari (US GP West), John Watson Penske (Austrian GP) and Andretti Lotus (Japanese GP). Ironically Niki Lauda had described the Nürburgring as the 'killer circuit' and inevitably 1976 was the last time it hosted the German GP, although it continued to be used by championship sports prototypes, GT and touring cars for several more years.

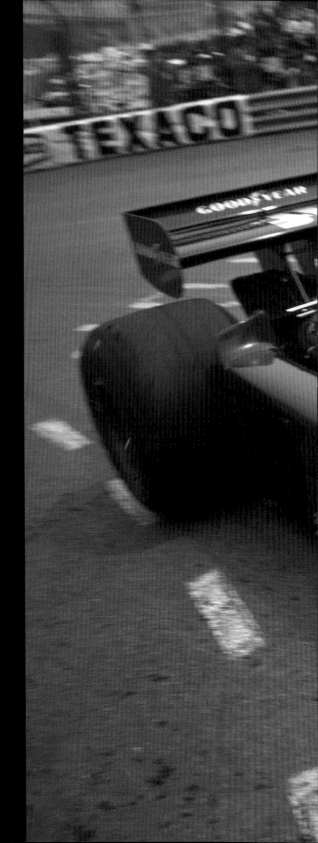

⬇ Patrick Depailler had been the first one to race the six-wheel Tyrrell P34, at Jarama where he retired, whilst Jody Scheckter waited until Zolder and finished fourth. At Monaco Jody was again out-qualified by the Frenchman but he finished ahead in the race. Depailler followed some 54sec behind, which was remarkable because a rear crossbeam had broken (as it did to Scheckter in Belgium) allowing one of the rear wheels gradually to lean in, but he survived to finish third. The second Ferrari of Regazzoni had nearly caught Scheckter before crashing out on lap 73. Mere inches away, Depailler's P34/2 – sans air-box and engine-cover, with the driver's arms visible through the cockpit side windows, which allowed sight of the front wheels – blasts past our intrepid photographer.

On 10 December 1975 McLaren and Marlboro announced the signing of James Hunt for 1976 to replace Emerson Fittipaldi, who had signed up to the Copersucar team. This is Fittipaldi Jr. in the latest Richard Divilia Copersucar FD-04 at Interlagos for the Brazilian GP where he qualified fifth fastest, but his race was ruined by a misfire and he finished 13th and three laps behind. Fellow Brazilian and teammate Ingo Hoffman finished 11th in the older FD-03, and with rare exception this was pretty much a precursor for the season. All was not well at Lotus either as Ronnie Peterson and Mario Andretti had found the new 77 troublesome during qualifying. Then in the race the two collided (shades of Kyalami '76), and subsequently Ronnie returned to March.

➡ The second GP of the year was at Kyalami (the Argentine GP had been cancelled because of economic and political problems). It was another Hunt/McLaren pole and another Lauda/Ferrari victory, but this time Hunt was but 1.3sec behind at the flag. Meanwhile, back in the ruck, here were the new for 1976 Alfa Romeo flat-12-powered Brabham BT45s for Carlos Reutemann, BT45-2 (left), and Carlos Pace, BT45-1 seen here. The Autodelta sports car-based engine offered 510bhp but it was a large, heavy, thirsty, and untidy unit that required more space and more fuel. Gordon Murray had been working on the new car since the middle of 1975 and they had finished 10th and 12th in Brazil, but both retired here early on with low oil pressure because of copious leaks.

⬅ When John Surtees temporarily withdrew from racing after the 1975 Austrian GP, John Watson found himself without a drive. However, at Watkins Glen he drove Roger Penske's new Penske PC3 and qualified mid-grid, but a misfire during the warm-up lap saw the PC1 (which was on a stand display) quickly recommissioned, and John drove it to ninth place as it was. The PC3 was the work of Geoff Ferris and Penske's American engineer Don Cox, who utilised the successful PC1 rear end for a car loosely based on the March 751, as can be seen. Watson started from the fourth row but only survived two laps before a split fuel line caught fire and the car was out. James Hunt had started from pole in the McLaren M23 but fell back with a misfiring engine, ultimately retiring when a sticking throttle caused him to crash, whilst Niki Lauda won for Ferrari ahead of Depailler (Tyrrell) and Pryce (Shadow).

Mario Andretti had returned to Vel's Parnelli Jones Racing after driving for Lotus in Brazil, but famous Indy-racer Jones did not share his co-founder Velco Miletich's enthusiasm for F1, and 1975 had not exactly been a success. By 1976 Andretti was keeping the team going, and at Kyalami the car was celebrating the bicentenary of the United States Declaration of Independence. Behind VPJ4/2 is the No. 6 Lotus 77-2 (or JPS 11 as Chapman preferred), which was driven by GP debutant Gunnar Nilsson, the team having replaced one Swede (Peterson) with another. The second car was handled by Bob Evans who had suffered the Stanley BRM in 1975, and both started right at the back (Nilsson last, in fact), finishing tenth and retired respectively. Andretti placed sixth at Kyalami in the VPJ4/2, but it was only to race once more, at Long Beach where Mario retired with a water leak. The team, which included former Lotus personnel Maurice Philippe, Andrew Ferguson, and Dick Scammell, was then disbanded, much to the dismay of everybody bar Mr Jones.

→ Alan Jones had resurrected his GP career by joining Team Surtees and was fresh from a second-place finish at the Brands Hatch ROC. At Brands the Durex-sponsored car ran unadorned, the BBC apparently having banned such overt advertising, and also allegedly being concerned about the public's sensibilities regarding condoms. Nick Brittan, in his outspoken *Autosport* 'Private Ear' column, noted that whilst motor sport was being castigated over visible sponsorship on screen, no such limitations extended to football and cricket. Fellow journo/BBC commentator Barrie Gill stated that, 'It's not the Beeb's idea. They are acting under pressure from the European Broadcasting Union. Advertising in all televised sports has got to be trimmed back.' This was perhaps allowing the BBC too much leeway, but even then it seems Britain was being dictated to and accepting it, at least for a while. Meanwhile, Jones in the still-unmarked TS19-02 qualified last and finished unclassified at the newly instigated US GP (West), whilst his Chesterfield-sponsored teammate, Brett Lunger, failed to qualify.

→ At Interlagos and Kyalami, Guy Ligier's new Matra V12-powered Ligier JS5-01, driven by Jacques Lafitte, retired. At Long Beach, however, happy Jacques finished fourth in what was dubbed 'the teapot' for obvious reasons. At the Spanish GP more new regulations, this time concerning air-boxes, ended this aesthetic abomination. The car was jointly the work of Matra's Gérard Ducarouge and Paul Carillo, together with Ligier's Michel Beaujon and Charles Deutsch of SERA (Société d'Etudes et de la Réalisation Automobile). It was sponsored by SEITA (Société Nationale d'Exploitation Industrielle des Tabacs et Allumettes), the then owners of Gitanes (gypsy women, hence the famous logo), the brand now being part of Imperial Tobacco. 1976, meantime, was fast becoming a Prancing Horse benefit, although at the US GP (West) at Long Beach it was Clay Regazzoni who won from Lauda, with Depailler third for Tyrrell after reportedly colliding with James Hunt.

◀ The idea of running a Monaco-style street race at Long Beach came from British travel agent Chris Pook, who worked there. In 1974 a huge investment programme for the city encouraged Pook to propose a race, and on 28 September 1975 the inaugural Grand Prix of Long Beach, for F5000 cars, was won by Brian Redman. The first F1 GP arrived in late March 1976, and this image captures the dramatic character of the circuit. Jody Scheckter (Tyrrell) and Jacques Lafitte (Ligier) are chased by Pace's Brabham, Mass's McLaren, Fittipaldi's Copersucar with Reutemann's Brabham on the inside, whilst at far left is Chris Amon's Ensign with Mario Andretti in the Parnelli VPJ4 alongside, followed by Stuck's March, Nilsson in the Lotus and Jones's Surtees. Note the crane-mounted mobile television camera hanging over the track just offline and the debris fencing.

◄ Pete Lyon's *Autosport* report of the Spanish GP at Jarama was headed 'Lauda's win, made to measure', in reference to Hunt's winning McLaren M23 that was disqualified for being too wide at the rear. Also excluded was the Ligier, but both cars were reinstated two months later, McLaren having argued that heat-generated rear tyre growth had caused the 1.8cm discrepancy. Lauda's second place was remarkable given that he was suffering two cracked ribs following a tractor accident. Much further down the field were the Frank Williams FW05s, née Hesketh 308C – the team now financed and controlled by Austrian-born Canadian oilman Walter Wolf. The set-up included the 308's designer Harvey Postlethwaite, but it was a structurally weak car with poor aerodynamics and made enormously overweight by necessary strengthening. Jacky Ickx and upcoming Michel Leclère stood no chance with it. Ickx finished seventh here following Hunt's reinstatement, but was later sacked after non-qualifying at the British GP. Later still, Frank Williams himself was removed, but he bounced back in 1977 with Patrick Head, as we shall see.

◄ Contrast the profile of the Lotus 77-1 (JPS 11) of Mario Andretti at Jarama. The 77s had been singularly unimpressive so far, but the cars now had a visibly lengthened wheelbase (as here) amongst other 'mods' and were performing much better as a result. In fact, Andretti was out-qualified by his Swedish No. 2 and followed him up the field to fifth place before stopping with a gear linkage failure. Nilsson went on to finish third on the road, which is what he was ultimately credited with after Hunt's successful appeal. Following the race, Tony Southgate left Shadow and joined Lotus, and gradually the car was improved.

➡️ Chris Amon had already raced Mo Nunn's Ensign N175 in Austria and Italy in 1975, but the team lost its HB Bewaking sponsorship and their newest car in 1976. So a revitalised Chris had to race the old 02 chassis, scoring a 14th place at Kyalami and an eighth at Long Beach. In Spain a new Dave Baldwin-designed LNF76 chassis 05 appeared, and Amon finished fifth. For the Belgian GP Chris was eighth-quickest in practice and duelled with Scheckter's six-wheel Tyrrell over fourth place, but crashed on lap 51 when the left rear wheel came adrift (Amon had noticed a slight vibration earlier on, perhaps because of the wheel coming loose). The car rolled twice, but happily Chris escaped with only heavy bruising. Once again note how immaculate the Ensign is. The Italian hegemony continued at Zolder, with Lauda winning from Regazzoni. Lafitte was third for Ligier, and Hunt retired, but circumstances were deceptive.

➡️ Famous F1 journalist and author Alan Henry shares a joke with Niki Lauda and Clay Regazzoni, who are reading *Motor News* at the Monaco GP. Once again it was a triumph for the Italian equine machines, with Lauda winning by 11sec from the two P34 Tyrrells of Scheckter and Depailler. At this stage Lauda had 51 points, and his nearest challenger was Regazzoni on 15 points, with the Tyrrell twins on 14 each, whilst Hunt (whose engine failed here) had a grand total of six (still without his Spanish GP points).

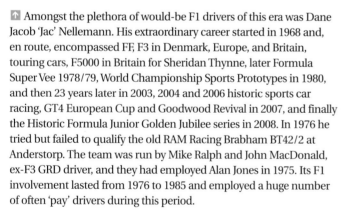

⬆ Amongst the plethora of would-be F1 drivers of this era was Dane Jacob 'Jac' Nellemann. His extraordinary career started in 1968 and, en route, encompassed FF, F3 in Denmark, Europe, and Britain, touring cars, F5000 in Britain for Sheridan Thynne, later Formula Super Vee 1978/79, World Championship Sports Prototypes in 1980, and then 23 years later in 2003, 2004 and 2006 historic sports car racing, GT4 European Cup and Goodwood Revival in 2007, and finally the Historic Formula Junior Golden Jubilee series in 2008. In 1976 he tried but failed to qualify the old RAM Racing Brabham BT42/2 at Anderstorp. The team was run by Mike Ralph and John MacDonald, ex-F3 GRD driver, and they had employed Alan Jones in 1975. Its F1 involvement lasted from 1976 to 1985 and employed a huge number of often 'pay' drivers during this period.

➡ The Tyrrells went one better in the Swedish GP at Anderstorp and finished 1/2 ahead of Lauda, Lafitte, and Hunt. Nevertheless, it was not quite so convincing as Mario Andretti, alongside pole sitter Scheckter, who had led the race and gained about 10sec on the Tyrrell, but around lap 30 the Lotus's motor began to fail and he retired on lap 45. Prior to this the American had reportedly been penalised one minute for jumping the start, but his retirement made this irrelevant. Mario in the Lotus 77-1 (JPS 11) leads away from the Tyrrells, Amon in the Ensign (who escaped unharmed after another big crash), Nilsson in the other Lotus, Lauda's Ferrari, and the rest.

⬆ It was at the French GP at Paul Ricard that Hunt's championship challenge finally gained momentum, helped by the reinstatement of his Spanish GP win. The car, too, which had lost its balance because of various changes, was back to full pace here after the team returned it to its Jarama specification. Hunt sat on pole but was out-dragged by Lauda. However, the McLaren was using a set of used tyres that gave it more consistent speed, and James was confident that the Ferrari's pace would falter as its 'new' rubber bedded in. This proved irrelevant as both Ferraris retired and Hunt drove to victory well clear of Depailler, Watson, and Pace. However, Watson's Penske was subsequently disqualified for a rear wing height infringement, so ultimately Andretti's Lotus ended up third ahead of Pace's Brabham. Hunt in his McLaren M23/8/2 leads Regazzoni's Ferrari 312T2/027, Peterson's March 761/3/2, and Depailler's Tyrrell P34/2.

⬅ The pressure is building at Brands Hatch, stoked by the partisan British press and crowd as Niki Lauda prepares to join the track during qualifying in his Ferrari 312T2/028. Behind him Clay Regazzoni in 027 is being waved on by the Ferrari mechanic. In the background one of the Martini Brabham-Alfas receives attention, and from this angle the pit lane actually seems quite wide.

➜ Divina Galica MBE, was the most successful female British skier ever, who competed in the 1964, 1968, 1972, and 1992 Winter Olympics, as well as being the fastest British woman on skis at 125mph. Her would-be F1 career was as a result of racing this Surtees TS16-05-03 in the domestic Shellsport G8 series. However, Galica's efforts, talent aside (she was quoted as saying at Brands, 'Look, let's face it, I was only a publicity stunt anyway. I mean I only started driving 18 months ago …'), were hampered by an inadequate budget and an uncompetitive car, and she failed to qualify at the British GP. This was her first attempt at GP racing and later there would be two more, equally unsuccessful for much the same reasons. The car was entered by Nick Whiting (a successful rallycross and saloon car racer in period), elder brother of Charlie Whiting (now the FIA Formula 1 Race Director). Nick, boss of All Car Equipe, seen here talking to Divina, with brother Charlie on the right, disappeared on 8 June 1990 along with five cars after a raid on his showroom. The cars were soon found, but it was only after a tip-off much later that Whiting's body was located in a shallow grave on Rainham Marshes, Essex, having been shot in the head.

◢ It was a very hot summer in 1976 and one can almost sense the build-up of testosterone in the crowd at the British GP, Brands Hatch. Does anybody recognise themselves here? The story of the first corner, first lap crash triggered by Regazzoni's Ferrari, Hunt's subsequent restart in a repaired car and passing Lauda's Ferrari to win confirms all our prejudices about 'rools and regs'. Hunt had technically committed an offence by not completing the red flag lap, having pulled off behind the pits to save driving his damaged car around the full lap. It ruled out Hunt, Regazzoni and Lafitte, and when the crowd heard this over the public address they exercised their collective lungs to the max. (Not everybody agreed, however, as one letter-writer to *Autosport* stated, 'I suspect that I was not alone in finding the displays of patriotism at Brands rather less than attractive.') This unnerved the management, and after much delay and inventive thinking Hunt was allowed back in (ditto Regazzoni and Lafitte), the delay enabling McLaren to repair the M23's steering and suspension. Following the race, Ferrari, Tyrrell, and Fittipaldi lodged protests over Hunt's restart, but the latter two withdrew and Ferrari's protest was rejected. Predictably, Ferrari then took the matter to the FIA International Court of Appeal and Hunt was disqualified two months later. So Lauda won anyway, ahead of Scheckter and John Watson's Penske.

⬆ If the British GP was controversial, the German GP was very nearly catastrophic, and events here finally ended the use of the 14.2-mile (22.85km) Nordschleife for F1. James Hunt started from pole ahead of his Austrian rival, but it was Jochen Mass who risked slicks with a light rain falling, his optimism driven by a patch of blue sky. Both Hunt and Lauda made poor starts, but the McLaren led on the drying road on this first lap, with Mass rising through the field from the fifth row. Then, on the second lap 12 cars, including Lauda's twitchy Ferrari, did not come round. He had crashed at Bergwerk, the wrecked Ferrari being touched by Edwards' Hesketh and hit heavily by Lunger's Surtees and Ertl's Hesketh. The race was stopped with Jochen Mass leading, and six cars did not make the restart. These included Amon's Ensign, Chris deciding that he was not happy with the emergency services' response time, which annoyed Mo Nunn. When it was restarted, Hunt led from flag to flag ahead of Scheckter and Jochen Mass. In the pits we see the Shadows of Jarier (DN5/4B but there are two identically numbered), closest to camera, and Pryce (DN5/5B), in the background, displaying their new Villiger Tabatip cigar livery. They finished 11th and 8th. Note the twin air-box intakes.

↗ Two weeks later the F1 teams assembled at an even more dangerous Österreichring, by which time Lauda's life-threatening injuries were public knowledge. Ferrari decided to boycott the race (not good news for the Austrian GP), apparently smarting over Hunt's Spanish GP reinstatement and then the British GP farce, which was still unsettled. Here is John Watson in the Penske PC4-001 (which had been first raced in Sweden) during practice, in which he was second-quickest behind Hunt's McLaren.

➡ There was an award ceremony at the Austrian GP for Arturo Merzario (stetson), Harald Ertl (hirsute), and Brett Lunger (looking normal) for their assistance in rescuing Niki Lauda from his blazing Ferrari at the Nürburgring.

The race for victory in Austria on a sometimes-wet track was won by John Watson in the Penske PC4-001 (which had been first raced in Sweden) from Lafitte's Ligier, Nilsson's Lotus (which expired on the slowing-down lap), and Hunt's ill-handling McLaren. Others contesting the podium included Scheckter, who crashed, and Peterson who finished sixth. At the start Watson just out-drags Hunt, with the rest following, and note Pryce's Shadow over the line on the left and Lafitte (Ligier) on the far right using the margins. After the season ended, the Penske PC4s were sold to ATS wheel manufacturer Günther Schmidt to race in 1977.

The Dutch GP followed Austria, and here James Hunt won his fifth GP to celebrate his 29th birthday, but only after a desperate struggle with Österreichring-victor John Watson until the Penske gearbox broke. The again ill-handling M23 was nearly caught by Regazzoni's sole Ferrari and Andretti's Lotus, whilst Tom Pryce started from third place on the grid in the new Shadow DN8/1A and finished a close fourth. Even more than Depailler, Pryce was an exciting man to watch, with a flamboyant driving style and huge speed, but like Tony Brise was fated never to reach his full potential. Tom has the Shadow on what must be full opposite lock here, a reminder of what racing used to be like, and a magnificent spectacle.

Even in 1976 there was still enough leeway for amateur drivers, by F1 standards, to enter a GP. Thus Austrian Otto Stuppacher, a Porsche and hill-climb racer, who had tried to enter the Austrian GP, but the authorities wisely declined. At Monza he was 14sec off the pace in the ÖSAC-entered Tyrrell 007/6, Jody Scheckter's 1975/76 car, but Watson and Hunt's times were disallowed because their fuel apparently exceeded the 101 maximum octane rating. This was just one of several little scrutineering 'problems' which backfired when Regazzoni's Ferrari fell foul of some ridiculous regulation. Anyway, with both McLarens and Watson's Penske disqualified (although they did start after Edwards and Merzario withdrew) Otto was now in the race, but by this time he had returned to Vienna. He tried again in Canada and America and predictably failed. As others have noted, very little is known of him and he soon disappeared into racing obscurity. Otto Stuppacher, 3 March 1947 – 13 August 2001.

All year Ronnie Peterson had been very fast in the March 761, but it was unreliable (he finished running in only four GPs and would not be back for 1977), had inadequate brakes, and wore its front tyres out when driven fast. March did not have the money to sort this out, but even so Ronnie led at Zandvoort and actually won the Italian GP, despite the chicanes. He leads Depailler and Scheckter (who had announced his decision to join the reconstituted Walter Wolf team for 1977) through the first of these obstructions on his way to victory at Monza, despite the antics of the officials who were trying to organise a Ferrari win. In the Maranello camp an obviously still unfit and badly burned Lauda turned up to race, no doubt influenced by Carlos Reutemann's presence, the Argentinian having departed from Brabham because of their unreliability. Niki, his Nomex balaclava red from his still-bleeding and raw skin finished a courageous fourth, whilst Regazzoni retired and Reutemann finished ninth.

The Canadian GP returned to Mosport in 1976 and James Hunt set fastest practice time, but in the race he let Ronnie Peterson lead for eight laps before assuming the lead himself and going on to win by 6sec from Depailler's Tyrrell and Andretti's improving Lotus 77-3/JPS 14. Scheckter was fourth, whilst poor Ronnie ended up ninth simply because the 761's shock absorbers were worn out, another victim of the team's penury. Ronnie leads away in the 761/6 from Hunt's M23/8/2, with Vittorio Brambilla's 761/1-4 just behind, which also faded away to finish 14th. As for the Ferraris, Regazzoni came sixth and Lauda eighth, whilst Reutemann sat out the rest of the year.

⬆ Jacky Ickx's F1 career had long been in decline and, like Chris Amon, whom he had replaced at Ensign, he found himself driving ever more third-rate machinery, culminating in the Williams/Hesketh hybrid in 1976. By contrast, the Ensign was a very good but underfunded car and Jacky retired in Holland, finished 10th at Monza, and 13th at Mosport, which did not match Amon's form. At Watkins Glen, Ickx started well back and then crashed on lap 14 after the Ensign N176/MN05 suddenly went out of control, hitting the Armco head-on, and yet again the nose of a car managed to find a gap, this time between the bottom rail and the ground. The front of the car, including the right side and fuel tank remained trapped, the fuel igniting, whilst the rest of it was ripped off, literally, as the remains ended up in the middle of the track, seen here. Ickx got away with minor burns, contusions, broken right foot/ankle, and hairline fractures in his left ankle, according to press reports. The race was another win for James Hunt ahead of the ever-competitive Scheckter, and Lauda finished third for Ferrari. Now, with all the nonsense behind them, Lauda led Hunt in the championship 68 to 65 points.

⬆ The first World Championship Japanese GP was held in the shadow of Mount Fuji and produced some very wet weather that made Niki Lauda retire after just two laps, declining to go any further. James Hunt, meanwhile, led most of the very delayed race (which many, including Hunt, did not want to start) until his wet-weather tyres wore out. He should have stopped earlier and he lost the lead on lap 62 to Depailler's Tyrrell, but he too was running out of rubber. Then Mario Andretti took over, and Hunt regained second as Depailler pitted. However, the McLaren's left front tyre finally failed and he was forced to pit for fresh tyres, rejoining in fifth place (not enough to win the title) with only five laps left. Ahead were Jones, Depailler and Regazzoni, in that order, but the Surtees and Ferrari developed punctures and Hunt passed them into third place, unaware that he now could win the championship. When he arrived back at the pits Hunt was raging, convinced that Teddy Meyer's management of the pit signals had cost him the race, but somebody finally got through to him – he was the new F1 World Champion. Both Colin Chapman and Mario Andretti in the Lotus 77-1 (JPS 11) seem concerned during practice and note the very complicated-looking front suspension.

➡ The Kojima KE007 was made by Matsuhisha Kojimi's company Kojima Engineering. Designed mainly by Masao Ono, who had drawn the lamentable Maki, this Cosworth-powered car was typically very stylised but surprisingly good. Driven by former motocross rider Masahiro Hasemi, who won the 1992 Daytona 24 Hours, it was by far the quickest of the Japanese entries and qualified on the fifth row alongside Ronnie Peterson. Running on Japanese Dunlop tyres, the car eventually finished 11th in the exacting race, although it had been overshadowed by Hoshino's old Tyrrell 007 that at one point was running third until the team ran out of tyres!

1977

PRANCING HORSE DEFEATS A WOLF

Niki Lauda became World Champion again in 1977 which was achieved through consistency rather than outright wins. His main rivals had too many retirements and Lauda beat Jody Scheckter in the new Wolf, Mario Andretti Lotus, Carlos Reutemann Ferrari and James Hunt McLaren. It was Andretti who had the most GP victories (four) whilst Lauda, Scheckter and Hunt scored three, Hunt's campaign compromised by McLaren's new M26, which was unreliable and Reutemann winning just the Brazilian race. The new Lotus 78 with its ground effect chassis was the superior car barring mechanical frailty whilst Tyrrell's radical P34 slipped backwards as its front tyre development faltered. Even with Ronnie Peterson driving it was no longer fully competitive. Brabham employed Carlos Pace again and John Watson but Pace died in a light aircraft accident early in the season whilst Watson had at least three potential winning drives which were lost to driver error, once, and car failure, twice. Renault appeared at Silverstone with the very first turbocharged GP car but it was to be a long road to success. Meanwhile F1's fatal accident tally rose again when a marshal ran across the road unsighted at Kyalami and was hit by the Tom Pryce's Shadow, killing both of them. Amidst the usual turmoil surrounding who drove for whom and why, the ever forthright Lauda decided to leave Ferrari before the Canadian GP. This was ostensibly in reaction to their decision to run Gilles Villeneuve thereby making it a three-car team. He was also disenchanted with Ferrari and moved to Brabham for a reported $1 million fee.

Unlike his successful forays elsewhere in motor sport, including F5000, a third at Indianapolis, and winning Le Mans in 1983, Vern Schuppan's F1 drives for BRM, Ensign, Graham Hill, and Surtees were a disappointment. F1 was always about having the best or second-best car, other than in wet weather, and the very talented Australian made the most of what he was given. This lovely shot at the Österreichring, where he finished 16th in the Austrian GP after a pit stop for tyres in the Team Surtees TS19-02, shows him having a 'real go', but alas to no avail and it was to be his final GP start.

Despite continuing economic and political upheaval the Argentine GP was back on the calendar for 1977. Alex-Dias Ribeiro was a Brazilian FF champion who made his mark racing in F3 and F2 before his first F1 drive at the 1976 US GP, Watkins Glen, finishing 12th. In 1977 he joined March, but it was a year of discord between team and driver with two eighth places the best result amongst a sea of DNQs and retirements starting here in Buenos Aires. Robin Herd already looks serious; Ribeiro qualified last but one, and retired because of gearbox problems. Note 761B/2's trademark March six-spoke wheels.

For 1977 there were driver changes aplenty. John Watson joined Brabham, replacing Carlos Reutemann, who had gone to Ferrari who had ousted Clay Regazzoni, the Swiss ending up at Ensign. Ronnie Peterson joined Depailler at Tyrrell, whilst Jody Scheckter was now driving for Wolf. Lastly, Vittorio Brambilla had left March for Surtees, whilst the Bicester concern was fielding Ribeiro and Ian Scheckter for now. Out of all this, the perhaps unlikely winner of the Argentine race was Jody Scheckter in the new Wolf WR1 ahead of Pace's Brabham and Reutemann's Ferrari. Hunt had been on pole but retired, and Watson led the race but also dropped out. A delighted Jody acknowledges the crowd under a very blue sky, the best possible beginning, and there was more to come.

In Brazil, Hunt was again the fastest in qualifying, a smidgeon quicker than Reutemann's Ferrari. In the race, James led, but the McLaren's front tyres were going off and Reutemann passed him whilst the McLaren pitted for fresh rubber. He then fought back to third place and slowly reeled in Tom Pryce's Shadow to reclaim second place, whilst the Shadow's engine broke. Niki Lauda finished third, a long way behind, but this status quo would soon be reversed, as Carlos did not win another GP in 1977. The Ferrari 312T2/029 is on its way to victory ahead of James Hunt and Jochen Mass (McLarens) and Andretti's Lotus – thus an Argentinian in an Italian car won the Brazilian GP, a true cosmopolitan result.

Tragedy awaited at the South African GP, Kyalami. On lap 21 Renzo Zorzi, Shadow's new driver for 1977, stopped his DN8/1A opposite the pits when a fuel line detached itself. It briefly caught fire and two marshals ran across the track with fire extinguishers, unsighted by oncoming cars because of the brow of the hill (seen here) at this point on the track. One just made it, but the second, 19-year-old Jansen van Vuuren, was struck by Tom Pryce's Shadow as he battled with Hans Stuck's March, the German having a lucky escape. Both were killed, the unfortunate Pryce (travelling at some 150mph) being hit on the head by the fire extinguisher that the young marshal had been carrying, and the car veered into the barriers and carried on under its own momentum before bouncing back into the path of Lafitte's Ligier, the Frenchman escaping with minor injuries. At the start of the race pole setter James Hunt, McLaren M23/11, leads Lauda, Ferrari 312T2/030, into Crowthorne ahead of the field. Hunt led for six laps and then Lauda took the lead to the finish as the McLaren struggled with grip finally falling back to fourth at the end. Jody Scheckter finished second and Patrick Depailler third in the Tyrrell despite being held up by Hunt for over half the race. Carlos Pace, Brabham BT45B (seen directly behind Lauda), finished 13th after stopping twice and then 13 days later perished in a light aircraft crash near São Paulo, Brazil.

The South African GP also saw the final race start of a BRM at a World Championship event. Australian Larry Perkins actually qualified the ancient P201B/04 and finished 15th. When the new P207 failed to show at the Brands Hatch ROC, Perkins walked away from the drive. Later on, Conny Andersson, Guy Edwards, and Teddy Pilette all tried and failed to make the grids in the newer P207. Note the almost hidden AUSTIN REED decal under the race number, this being a well known clothing and suit retailer in the UK.

Mario Andretti looking pensive as he joins his Lotus 78-3 on the grid at Long Beach for the US GP (West) beside Lauda's pole-position Ferrari. The 78 was new for 1977 and had been drawn by Ralph Bellamy. It was the first 'ground effect' car and Andretti led more race laps with it during the season than any other car/driver. The race was led by Jody Scheckter for 76 of 80 laps, but the Wolf WR1 had a slowly deflating right front tyre, and with four laps to go Andretti took the lead to win the race, whilst Jody was also overtaken by Lauda's Ferrari, so the disappointed South African finished third. Equally demorialised was Jacques Lafitte (Ligier JS7) who occupied fourth position at Long Beach for much of the race, and then the electrical cut-out switch mounted on the steering wheel failed with just two laps left. Merde! There had also been a first-lap accident caused by Reutemann's Ferrari, which eliminated Brambilla, Lunger, and Reutemann, whilst Hunt survived being airborne and raced on to finish seventh.

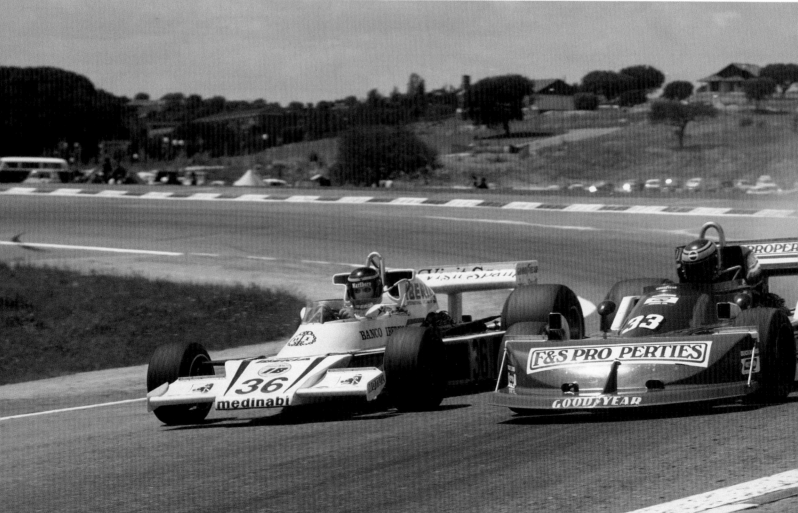

⬉ Behind the front-runners at Long Beach Emerson Fittipaldi was continuing his attempts to make the Fittipaldi FD04-03 go quicker, and he succeeded here by qualifying seventh fastest. He went even better in the race and finally came home fifth, the car having previously benefitted from some suspension tweaks, courtesy of Maurice Philippe.

⬅ The Iberia Airlines-sponsored McLaren M23/6 of Emilio de Villota and Boy Hayje's F&S Properties March 761/3 during practice at Jarama for the Spanish GP. Dutchman Hayje had raced the old Penske PC3 in the 1976 Dutch GP and contested a part season in 1977, only qualifying at the South African and Belgian GPs, and his F1 aspirations ended at Zandvoort. A sometime bank manager for Banco Iberia, de Villota was sponsored by his former employers (imagine the headlines if that happened today) and he started on the penultimate row and finished 13th. The rest of his seven-race F1 season was a bust with five DNQs and a collision with the course car in Austria. He appeared once in 1978, again at Jarama (DNQ), then in 1981 a DNS here, followed by five DNQs in 1982. His true comfort level was in the British F1 Aurora FX series, finishing third in 1979 and winning the championship in 1980.

⬆ Derek Gardner's unique creation was already beginning to lose its competitive edge and Ronnie Peterson was finding himself being outpaced by teammate Depailler. The 1977 Tyrrell P34 had grown larger and heavier, but more pertinently Goodyear were not developing the rubber for its 10in-diameter front wheels, one of the hazards of being radically different. Ronnie finished eighth after following Depailler, who retired, whilst Mario Andretti won his second GP in a row well clear of Reutemann's Ferrari and Scheckter's Wolf. World Champion Hunt raced the new McLaren M26/1 but the car had developed a misfire and he was out after 11 laps.

◄ A moment of peace and contentment away from the madness for James Hunt with his beloved dog Oscar in Marbella, where Hunt lived in between races.

◄ An uneasy alliance. Niki Lauda and Carlos Reutemann stroll past the restaurant at La Rascasse before the race in Monte Carlo. Lauda had not been sympathetically received by Ferrari following his recovery, and the Austrian was determined to show who was boss in the team. Although out-qualified by Carlos, Niki finished second, and the Argentinian, with grip problems, was third at Monaco, whilst Jody Scheckter won a second GP for Wolf and also provided Cosworth with its 100th GP victory. Just over Reutemann's left shoulder can be seen Rupert Keegan in his second GP start (he finished 12th), and I wonder who the man with the No. 090 STANDS-PITS pass is.

► This is Austrian Hans Binder, whose F1 CV started with one-off drives in 1976 with Ensign, and later Walter Wolf, and continued into 1977 with Surtees and, post Monaco, with ATS (three races), then back to Surtees for the remaining GPs. There was one more attempt at the 1978 Austrian GP with ATS, which resulted in a DNQ and an end to his F1 drives. Binder, with his beautiful companion, looks happy enough in his Durex-sponsored Surtees TS19-01, even though he was starting from the back with Rupert Keegan's Hesketh. The Austrian retired on lap 35.

⬆ The wet/dry/wet Belgian GP at Zolder began with pole sitter Mario Andretti and John Watson retiring on lap one after Andretti touched the Brabham and both cars crashed out. Niki Lauda led until 20 laps from the end, when he was overtaken by Gunnar Nilsson for the Swede's first, and only, GP win. Fellow Swede Ronnie Peterson finished third in the Tyrrell P34, and Vittorio Brambilla was fourth for Surtees. World Champion Hunt chose the wrong tyres and ended up seventh. Here, Nilsson in the Lotus 78-2 passes David Purley's Mike Pilbeam-designed LEC CRP-1. David had made his reappearance in F1 at the Spanish GP and posted a DNQ, but at Zolder when most of the cars changed to dry tyres when it briefly stopped raining, Purley stayed out and led the race for a while.

↗ A face from the past and one forgotten by many. Born 17 May 1948, Mikko Kozarowitsky was a Finnish driver whose career began in Formula Vee in 1968, progressing to F3 in 1970, then military service before racing Formula Super Vee in 1974/75 in Europe and America, thence to an unsuccessful interlude in F2 in 1975/76. His F1 experience was limited as a pay driver and he attempted to qualify the RAM Racing/F&S Properties March 761/8 at the Swedish GP. He failed through lack of testing and unfamiliarity with the uncompetitive car, which had been Brambilla's 1976 spare. At Silverstone he failed again when he crashed and injured his hand during pre-qualifying while avoiding a collision with Rupert Keegan. The team allegedly wanted him to try to qualify another car, but he refused and never raced again.

➡ After coming close on occasion, Jacques Lafitte scored his first GP win at Anderstorp in the very smooth-looking Ligier JS7-02. This time, instead of Lafitte, it was Andretti's Lotus that ran into last-minute problems, having led all the way bar lap one and then having to pit with three laps to go with a fuel metering unit fault, finally finishing sixth. In between, a big battle featuring Hunt, Depailler, Reutemann, Lafitte, Mass, and Watson, the last named having survived a first-lap collision with Scheckter's Wolf, which retired. As above they finished 12th, 4th, 3rd, 1st, 2nd and 5th. It was the first time that a French-built and powered car with a French driver had won a World Championship GP. Lafitte is greeted after the race by the joyous Ligier crew and Guy Ligier running round the back of the car – even Teddy Meyer, at right with headphones and mike, is smiling.

⬆ Dijon-Prenois had been lengthened to 2.36 miles (3.8km) but it was still only a 73sec lap for the quickest cars at the French GP. The story of the race was simply Andretti on pole, but Watson leading right up to the final lap when he was undone by his wretched car running out of fuel. John still finished a close second, but surely nobody other than Chris Amon had such ill fortune at this level. James Hunt finished third in the McLaren M26. Here are Watson in the Brabham BT45B-6 and Andretti in the Lotus 78-3 going at it hammer and tongs before the gremlins struck.

↗ There were over 40 entries for the British GP at Silverstone, of which 14 had to pre-qualify on the Wednesday before the race. Amongst them was Australian Brian McGuire, who came to England with Alan Jones back in the early 1970s to race in F3. During 1976 he bought the 1975 Williams FW04 and tried to race in the British GP, but he was a reserve entry and not allowed to compete. The car was 'updated' in 1977 and renamed the McGuire BM-1 and Brian attempted to get into the British GP with it. This was doomed to fail, but again we see how much more flexible, if more dangerous, F1 used to be. After this, McGuire went back to competing in the Shellsport G8 series, but at the August Bank Holiday Brands Hatch meeting a mechanical failure caused the car to crash at Stirling's. It somersaulted off the track on to a marshals' post killing two of its inhabitants and the unfortunate driver. Brian McGuire, 13 December 1945 – 29 August 1977.

➡ David Purley's F1 adventure began in Monte Carlo in 1973, contesting five championship rounds, ending at Monza. In 1974 he failed to qualify the Token at the British GP at Brands Hatch, and then returned in 1977 as already stated. During pre-qualifying for the British GP his LEC's engine caught fire in the pits and was quickly extinguished, but the dry powder foam had formed a slippery coating on the throttle slides. When he rejoined the track the throttles stuck open approaching Woodcote, and he went off hitting the wall at 108mph (174kph) and stopped within 26in (66cm), surviving an estimated deceleration of 179.8g, thought to be the highest g-force ever survived by a human being. He returned to racing in the British Aurora F1 series in 1979 but eventually perished in a flying accident when he crashed his Pitts Special Aerobatic biplane into the sea off Bognor Regis, Sussex, where he had been born. David Charles Purley, 26 January 1945 – 2 July 1985.

↑ It was James Hunt who insisted that Gilles Villeneuve be given a chance in F1 after the Canadian beat Hunt in a Formula Atlantic race in Canada. He duly qualified ninth (having waltzed through pre-qualifying) less than a second off Hunt's pole time in the newer M26, raced seventh and finished 11th in his older M23/8 after stopping with apparent overheating, which turned out to be a faulty temperature gauge. Up at the front his World Champion teammate was held at bay for 49 laps by John Watson until the Brabham's fuel pressure relief valve broke. He was quoted as saying, 'I've never heard of that happening to a racing car before.' This was Hunt's first GP win of the year, ahead of the omnipresent Lauda, with Nilsson's Lotus in third.

↗ Not for the first time was an opportunistic driver tempted to race when he had not qualified during practice. In this instance it is famous 1974 European Touring Car champion and Porsche-racer Hans Heyer, who was third-reserve at the German GP, Hockenheim, in Günther Schmidt's hybrid ATS-Penske PC4-001. The cars were always beautifully presented but rarely competitive, and the team's temperamental boss probably did not help. Heyer lasted nine laps having been black-flagged, but he retired anyway with a broken gearbox.

→ The Harvey Postlethwaite-designed Wolf WR1 had been a success, and if Scheckter finished a race it was usually at the front. By the time of the German race it was chassis WR3, in which he started from pole position, but the race was dominated by Lauda's Ferrari and Jody had to settle for second, being slightly hampered by falling fuel pressure. Hans Stuck, who had replaced Pace at Brabham, finished an excellent third in the Martini Brabham BT45B, a result he would repeat in Austria. Note the paper caught in the side radiator and the brace of Lotus 78s in the background that had retired earlier on after blowing up. (Lotus had use of Cosworth's special development motors that were prone to self-destruct.) Hockenheim was very hard on engines in its original long form, and Teddy Meyer remarked after driving round the track, '... I never realised what it was – a couple of autobahns and a stadium!'

 1977 was the year of white cars (Surtees, Shadow and Ensign) and at the Austrian GP Arturio Merzario temporarily replaced Ricardo Patrese at Shadow. This was because the team's sponsor Ambrosio had not been paying their dues, and Patrese was contracted to both the team and the sponsor. He was back for the Dutch GP, and meanwhile Alan Jones in the other Shadow won the race, thanks to a canny tyre choice and the Australian's ever improving form. Merzario qualified 22nd and retired with a gear change problem in the DN8/5A. That summer Tony Southgate had returned to the team, and this was reflected in the cars' performances. Lauda, Hunt and Andretti led the grid with the Austrian finishing second whilst the latter two both led the race before retiring.

 The Dutch GP turned into a Lauda v. Lafitte (Ferrari flat-12 v. Matra V12) battle that the Austro-Italian combination won but not by much from Scheckter's Wolf. However, for the first five laps it had been Hunt at the front leading Andretti, but then they collided, each blaming the other and both retiring. The latest F1 'sensation' was Patrick Tambay driving Teddy Yip's Theodore Racing Ensign N177/MN08, whilst Clay Regazzoni had been racing the works car. Tambay began his F1 career with a DNQ at Paul Ricard for Team Surtees, but had switched camps for the British GP. He retired, but at Hockenheim finished a notable sixth, then retired in Austria. At Zandvoort he climbed to third place from 12th on the grid by lap 35 and then ran out of fuel with two laps to go, being finally classified fifth.

◤ Not the sharpest image, but irresistible, as Ronnie Peterson winds on the opposite lock on those tiny front wheels in the Tyrrell P34/6. He out-qualified Depailler by just 0.01sec at Monza and finished sixth in the Italian GP, whilst the Frenchman retired with a blown engine. Mario Andretti won his fourth and final GP of the year whilst Lauda's second place virtually guaranteed him the drivers' championship. Tyrrell, meantime, were saying goodbye to Derek Gardner at the end of the season. He was going to be Divisional Director of Engineering and Research of Borg-Warner in Letchworth, Hertfordshire. His replacement was ex-Lotus and Vels Parnelli designer Maurice Philippe.

◀ Another unlikely F1 driver was the Swiss saloon car racer and garage proprietor Loris Kessel, whose unsuccessful tenure at RAM Racing in 1976 had ended in legal conflict. In 1977 he entered the Apollon-Williams FW-03 at Monza under the auspices of the Jolly Club of Switzerland. It was driven by Merzario in 1974 and briefly 1975, then subsequently by Brise, Magee, Ian Scheckter, Migault, Ashley, Vonlanthen and Renzo Zorzi. Kessel had brought it here in 1976, but did not take part in practice, and it turned up again in 1977, but it was too slow although not the slowest as that honour fell to Giorgio Francia, who very briefly drove one of the Martini Brabhams. Kessel predictably did not qualify the car that has apparently broken down in the pit entrance road and it was his final F1 appearance.

▲ Niki Lauda finished fourth and secured the 1977 World Championship whilst James Hunt won the US GP (East) at Watkins Glen with an optimum set-up for the wet track, which lasted long enough for his rain tyres not to wear out as the track dried. He beat Andretti's dry set-up but wet-tyre-shod Lotus, with Scheckter's Wolf in third (again). Further down the order was Jean-Pierre Jabouille in the Renault Elf RS01-1, which had made its debut at the British GP where it retired, as it did at every race it had attended thereafter, Zandvoort, Monza, and here. The car was very tricky in the wet, courtesy of its turbocharger, and it stopped with alternator failure on lap 30. At its final outing of the year in Canada the car failed to qualify.

⬆ James Hunt harried Mario Andretti for the lead of the Canadian GP for 60 laps and slipped by when Andretti was baulked by Jochen Mass in the other McLaren. However, when Mass slowed down to let his teammate through, Hunt hit him and crashed out of the race, whilst Mass spun but would eventually take third place. Safe in the lead, Andretti's motor blew with just two laps to go, which allowed Jody Scheckter to win for Wolf, their third GP victory of 1977, ahead of Depailler's Tyrrell. Behind all this was Hawaiian-born Danny Ongais, former drag racer and F5000 driver for Ted Field's Interscope Racing, who were running their Penske PC4 again as they had at Watkins Glen where Ongais spun off. It was a new car, chassis 003, built in the Penske workshops to the same specification as the 1976 Austrian GP winning car. Unfortunately, it did not shine at Mosport, even if its smart black paintwork did, and Ongais finished seventh but two laps behind.

↗ The 17th and final race of the year was the Japanese GP at Fuji, and this time it was dry and sunny. Two JPS Lotus 78s were entered but Nilsson's chassis 78-4 was wearing Imperial International red colours rather than the familiar JPS black and gold. He qualified 14th and retired on lap 63 with gearbox failure. It was his final GP. Gunnar's excellent race form had fallen away in the second half of the season and he began to feel ill, complaining that he was in pain when tightening up his crutch straps and was diagnosed with testicular cancer later in the year. Even so, he signed to drive for the new Arrows team in January 1978, but it was never going to be and he died in October. Gunnar Nilsson, 20 November 1948 – 20 October 1978.

➡ James Hunt's GP-winning days came to an end here in Fuji, Japan, where he scored one of his most apparently effortless wins in the McLaren M26/3 by leading from start to finish. It was his tenth GP victory and few would have believed it was his last. He started alongside pole-man Mario Andretti, who let his revs drop away, which was why he was eighth on the first lap. Uncharacteristically, he misjudged driving round the outside of Lafitte's Ligier on lap two and hit the French car's rear left wheel with his right front, which broke the 78's steering arm. The Lotus hit the barriers hard and Andretti was out, fortunately uninjured. Carlos Reutemann was second for Ferrari, Patrick Depailler third for Tyrrell, and Alan Jones had another good race in the Shadow for fourth place. During the race, Gilles Villeneuve, who had joined Ferrari, collided with Peterson's Tyrrell and his car cleared the barriers and mowed down many people in a prohibited area. Gilles was unhurt, but a marshal and a photographer were killed, and others seriously injured. So ended another year of triumph, tragedy, and failure.

1978

A RADICAL DESIGN TOO FAR

The accolade for the most radical F1 car of 1978 fell to Gordon Murray's extraordinary 'fan car' the Brabham BT46B whose fan sucked the rear of the car to the ground. It appeared at the Swedish GP where Lauda won but as the fan was deemed to be a moveable aerodynamic device which was not allowed it was never used again. Brabham's season with Lauda, John Watson and later Nelson Piquet provided two wins for Lauda and several podiums. Otherwise Mario Andretti and Ronnie Peterson, second time at Lotus, had an insurmountable advantage over the rest and Andretti won six races (five with the new 79 and one with the older type 78) and the World Championship. Ronnie won two races, one with the older 78, and finished runner-up in the World Championship but he had died after complications from an accident at Monza. Ferrari and Carlos Reutemann scored four GP wins but the now Michelin-shod cars were inconsistent and Villeneuve had a poor season. Tyrrell continued with Depailler and newcomer Didier Pironi and Patrick won at Monaco in the new Tyrrell 008. The indefatigable Frank Williams, who had set up Williams Engineering in 1977 with Patrick Head, appeared with the new FW06 and Alan Jones and car and driver were competitive if unreliable although Jones did finish second in the US GP (East). Arrows arrived on the grids comprised of Shadow's senior personnel, which caused much discontent and their driver Ricardo Patrese was wrongly blamed for causing Peterson's Monza accident. McLaren suffered a disastrous season with poor cars, Hunt began to lose interest and the promising Patrick Tambay was demoralised. Wolf Racing retained Scheckter but their best results were a brace of second places whilst Renault continued to be unreliable. Finally Team Surtees disappeared from F1 unable to find sufficient funding to continue.

⬇ Jean-Pierre Jarier had led the Canadian GP for many laps in the Lotus 79 followed by Jones, Scheckter and Villeneuve but by lap 25 Villeneuve was leading the chase ahead of Scheckter, and Jones. When Jarier retired, Villeneuve was left in the lead and finished 14sec ahead of Scheckter, with the other Ferrari of Reutemann third. Here, Gilles in the Ferrari 312T3/034 surfs the waves, well almost, on the way to his first GP victory at the last race of 1978.

⬆ Much of the entry for the opening round of the 1978 F1 World Championship were identifiably existing cars from 1977, but March had left F1. The exceptions were Brabham with a new tidied-up BT45C chassis, but the only completely new machines were the Patrick Head-designed Williams FW06, Maurice Philippe's Tyrrell 008, and the ATS HS-1, of which more later. Drivers had swapped around: Peterson was back with Lotus, Didier Pironi made Tyrrell all French, Patrick Tambay had joined McLaren, Lauda had exchanged flat-12s and gone to Brabham, Regazzoni and Hans Stuck were casting Shadows, Mass was ATS-mounted, and so on. The big news was that Michelin were providing tyres for Ferrari. For now, however, it was as before concerning race form, with Andretti winning the GP convincingly in last year's car. Lauda's Brabham-Alfa finished second, and Depailler's new Tyrrell third. Pictured in the Williams FW06/1 is Alan Jones, who raced mid-field until retiring – a false indication of what was to come.

↗ There had been a management exit from Shadow in late 1977 – Tony Southgate, Alan Rees, Jackie Oliver, and Dave Wass set up the Arrows team with backing from Franco Ambrosio, who had previously sponsored Shadow. The new car, known as the FA1, would later be outlawed by court order (and the four existing cars dismantled), a judge having found in favour of Don Nichols (founder of Shadow) observing that FA1 it could not have been designed and built without reference to existing Shadow DN9 plans. For now, however, all looked good, and Ricardo Patrese raced the new car in Brazil, reaching eighth place despite a pit stop, and finally finishing tenth after stopping again for fuel and tyres. The Brazilian GP (held this year at Rio de Janeiro) continued the class of '77 theme with Carlos Reutemann winning for Ferrari in the 312T2 from Fittipaldi's Fittipaldi, and Lauda's Brabham-Alfa third.

➡ The Copersucar was now known as the Fittipaldi, and during 1977 Dave Baldwin had designed the F5 but departed before the car was raced in the French GP. For their 1978 car the Fittipaldis engaged Giacomo Caliri's Fly Studio in Modena (Caliri had been a Ferrari F1 engineer) to turn the F5 into a 'wing car', and this was the result, the F5A. It was an immediate and significant improvement over the previous cars and, after some practice woes, Emerson Fittipaldi would claim second place in Brazil, the team's best ever result, but despite some further consistent top six finishes (two fourths, two fifths, and one sixth) during 1978, which was their best year, the car/driver combination was never a winning prospect.

At Kyalami the Arrows cars were painted in German brewer Warsteiner's colours, and Patrese had been joined by Rolf Stommelen, every German sponsor's favourite driver, apparently. Patrese famously led the race for 37 laps in No. 35 (FA1/2), which caused a furore before his engine blew up, whilst Stommelen in No. 36 (FA1/1) finished ninth. Victory fell to Ronnie Peterson's Lotus 78 on the last lap after Depailler's leading Tyrrell developed a smoking engine (finishing second), with John Watson a close third despite spinning on an oil slick.

The Ferraris were now T3s, and at the US GP (West) at Long Beach they occupied the front row, Reutemann two-tenths quicker than Villeneuve. The meteoric Canadian led the first 37 laps before colliding with Regazzoni's Shadow, leaving a slower-starting Reutemann to win the race ahead of Andretti's Lotus and Depailler's Tyrrell. Note the elevated broadcasting camera position. As ever with Gilles, you only need the picture, no words are really required. Suffice it to say that this is the Michelin-shod Ferrari 312T3/034 up on tiptoe with opposite lock applied on the brow of a steep drop.

Patrick Depailler had thus far finished third, retired, second, and third in the first four races of 1978, and at Monaco he would achieve his maiden GP victory with the Tyrrell 008/3. This was long overdue, but success is often a stranger to those who most deserve it, as per John Watson who led the race in the Martini Brabham-Alfa until braking problems sent him down the chicane escape road. John recovered to finish fourth, with Scheckter's Wolf WR1 third and Lauda, in the other Brabham, second.

Like so many others, Rupert Keegan's F1 career was severely compromised by uncompetitive cars and, hyperbole aside, it is impossible to know how good he could have been. His father owned British Air Ferries and sponsored Rupert's racing, and following a successful 1976 F3 season he found himself racing the Penthouse Rizla Hesketh 308E in 1977, a grid-filler at best. Nevertheless, Rupert qualified it at every race, with a best finish of seventh in Austria. In 1978 he joined the struggling Team Surtees for its final year in racing and suffered five DNQs, two non-starts, five retirements, and one finish (11th in Spain). At Monaco, Rupert out-qualified Fittipaldi and Stommelen, but the car only lasted eight laps before a crown-wheel-and-pinion failure. Compare the frontal aspect of the TS19-02 with the Tyrrell, and again notice how much roll some period F1 cars generated as Keegan negotiates the harbourside barriers.

→ Former Super Renault and F2 star, the extremely fast René Arnoux was the chosen driver for Automobiles Martini's DFV-powered Martini Mk23 F1 project. The Martini was the creation of Tico Martini, who built these rapid devices in his workshops at Magny-Cours. Arnoux had failed to qualify it in South Africa and Monte Carlo, but at Zolder he was comfortably on the grid ahead of some respectable names, and he finished ninth. After this the Martini finished 14th in France, did not qualify for the British and German races, finished ninth in Austria, and retired from the Dutch GP. Martini then wisely dropped the project as F1 headed ever more into the space age. René, meanwhile, saw out the season in North America for Team Surtees in its dying days.

→ Chapman's latest F1 creation, the Lotus 79, was finally raced at Zolder by Mario Andretti (who had decided not to go to Indy) and having been eight-tenths quicker than Reutemann's Ferrari in practice simply drove away and won the Belgian GP. His task was made easier by the fact that teammate Peterson was still in the 'old' 78, that there was a chaotic start (with Hunt, Lauda, and Fittipaldi eliminated by grid accidents), that Reutemann's Ferrari was understeering, and that Villeneuve (who had been in second place) had to pit for a new front tyre. The race was a Lotus 1/2, as witnessed by the team's joyous faces, with Reutemann third and Villeneuve fourth. Chapman has jumped the wall and is standing on the live track, whilst behind the barrier are Ronnie's wife Barbro, Bob Dance (Lotus chief mechanic), Nigel Bennett (chief cace cngineer), and Glenn Waters (Lotus mechanic).

← The Spanish GP was out of place in the calendar this year, and at Jarama there were two Lotus 79s, which produced another 1/2. Andretti started from pole alongside Peterson (they had nearly a second in hand over the rest) and took the lead on lap six from a fast-starting James Hunt, whilst Ronnie recovered from a poor start to finish second. In picture, the typically focused and busy Chapman is plugged into the car, whilst kneeling on the right is our friend 'Schleg' again.

↑ In 1978, both McLaren and their star driver started to go into decline. Having got the M26 up to speed, with Hunt driving, the issue became the temperament of James, whose lifestyle and attitude was not appropriate for the situation. Insiders believed he was no longer fully committed, but the cars were not as competitive as they had been during the M23 years. Nevertheless, Hunt led the Spanish GP for five laps, then occupied second place until lap 51, dropping to fourth as his tyres deteriorated, stopping on lap 60 for new rubber, and finally coming in sixth. During practice the McLaren appeared with this suspension-mounted front wing (that had already been tried during testing at Donington) in an attempt to cure the M26's understeering tendency on race rubber, but Hunt decided not to use it. The M26/3 cruises past John Watson's Brabham BT46-4, which finished fifth in the race with gear selection problems.

When looking at this picture I am reminded of a very vulgar and ancient joke, as well as a period Hoover advertisement with the punchline 'It beats as it sucks as it cleans.' Innovation, it seems, was not the sole perquisite of Messrs Chapman, Wright, Rudd, Aldridge, Southgate, et al. Gordon Murray could be even more radical, although not original given the 1970 Chaparral 2J. The Brabham 'fan car' raced once, won, and was then tactfully withdrawn after being declared illegal. Niki Lauda drove BT46/2-2/6 to victory in the Swedish GP, whilst Andretti's motor expired. In the background the COC (Cessna Owners Club) enjoys the Scandinavian sunshine. Behind the Austrian Ricardo Patrese continued his impressive form by finishing second a mere 0.086 of a second ahead of Ronnie Peterson. However, Ronnie had pitted to change a punctured rear tyre on lap 12 dropping to 17th and spent the rest of the race catching up, afterwards complaining that the Italian had been weaving about like an F3 driver.

By mid-1978 the Wolf WR1-4 series cars were becoming outdated, and Harvey Postlethwaite produced the WR5/6 duo, an ugly, angular design that appeared at Monaco but was not raced, retired in Belgium, finished fourth in Spain, retired in Sweden, and finished sixth here at Paul Ricard. Jody sits in WR5/2 on the fourth row of the grid with team-owner Walter Wolf on the left side-pod and team-manager Peter War (in cap, headphones, and glasses) on the other side. The car and driver would go on to retire in Britain, finish second in Germany, retire in Austria, 12th in the Dutch and Italian GPs, before finishing off with a third and second in America and Canada.

Behind the perhaps inevitable Lotus 1/2 in favour of Mario again, James Hunt scored his last ever World Championship points by finishing third at Paul Ricard in his regular M26/3. Having disposed of John Watson, seen here following, Hunt had not given up on winning. He was right on Peterson's tail with one lap left, but was suffering from the extreme heat and feeling very nauseous, finally being sick inside his helmet, and he spun as a result but still made it home.

◥ It is frustrating that a man who had been a FF champion in the mid-1970s, raced a works Chevron in F3, was a star of the domestic Aurora F1 series, and won the Macau GP twice – usually a sure pointer to stardom – should struggle to get into F1. Geoff Lees was later to drive for Tyrrell, once in 1979, for Shadow in 1980 and twice in 1982, once for Theodore and once for Lotus. Lees, meanwhile, tried but failed to qualify the Mario Deliotti Ensign N176/MN05 (the 1976 works car driven by Amon, Binder, Neve, and Ickx) at Brands Hatch. His attempts were further hindered by wrecking the Ensign's nose on the back of Hunt's McLaren, which had apparently braked coming out of Paddock Hill bend.

◄ This is the determined Tony Trimmer, former FF winner and 1970 British F3 champion who tried to qualify the Makis four times between the 1975 German GP and the 1976 Japanese GP. In 1977 he tried again with a Surtees TS19 at Silverstone and one last time with the Melchester Racing McLaren M23 at the 1978 British GP. It was an ex-Brett Lunger car, M23/14. He was also one of the regular Aurora AFX stars, but like Lees did not have a pot of gold, and this was his last attempt at GP racing.

◥ Back in the ruck at Brands Hatch are Bruno Giacomelli in the third works McLaren M26/7, the Shadow DN9/1A of Clay Regazzoni with his teammate Hans Stuck in DN9/4A hidden behind the M26, and the Tyrrell 008/5 of Didier Pironi visible. Bruno, known as Jack O'Malley for obvious reasons, was a well-funded F2 ace who had made his first GP appearance at the 1977 Italian GP for McLaren. He finished seventh here, Regazzoni retired, Stuck, after spinning on the first lap, was a notable fifth, and Pironi also retired. As did both Lotus 79s and Hunt, so Carlos Reutemann won the race just ahead of Niki Lauda, and John Watson was third. One Ferrari, two Brabhams, and three flat-12s.

⬆ One of the old series Wolf, in this case WR3, was raced at the German GP by future World Champion Keke Rosberg, who had entered F1 in 1978. It was owned by 'Teddy' Yip's Theodore Racing team, which had also produced their own car earlier in the season. At Hockenheim, Keke qualified the car far back and finished tenth, whilst the race winner was, yes, Mario Andretti, but Peterson retired after setting fastest lap. Scheckter finished second, and Jacques Lafitte brought the Ligier JS9 home in third place.

↗ At Hockenheim, Nelson Piquet had started his F1 career with the works Ensign, but in Austria he had moved on to the B&S Fabrications McLaren M23/11, American Brett Lunger's spare car. This is probably a practice shot, as Piquet was one of the victims of the first start, which was dry and then it rained sending the slick-shod cars spinning off all round the circuit. At Monza he finished ninth in the McLaren, but a drive with Brabham awaited in Canada after four GP starts comprising three retirements and that one ninth place.

➡ In Austria, Ronnie Peterson, let off the leash, won as he pleased some 50sec clear of Patrick Depailler's Tyrrell, whilst Andretti crashed during the first seven-lap race that had been abandoned because of a downpour. This was the Swede's tenth GP victory, and his last.

⬆ At the Dutch GP, Zandvoort Ronnie was back in place and he finished 2nd behind Mario Andretti. On the first lap of the race Didier Pironi (Tyrrell) and Ricardo Patrese (Arrows), seen here, collided. Of course there were no 'safety cars' in those days and the drivers merely slowed down whilst the wreckage was removed. Despite three more full seasons in F1 (1979/80/81) and two starts in 1982 (Williams and Ferrari), Mario never won another GP but he was on his way to becoming the 1978 World Champion, only the second ever American to achieve this to this day.

➡ Ronnie Peterson in his Lotus 79-2 during practice at the Italian GP with Bob Dance on the right front wheel. He had enjoyed some great times at Monza, finishing second in 1971, and winning it three times (1973/74 and 1976). He came to the 1978 Italian GP lying second in the drivers' championship, and then during Sunday practice he crashed his Lotus 79. There was only one other 79, which was Mario's spare car, so he used the old 78 for the race, which did not have the front end structural integrity of the later car that might have saved him from such serious leg injuries. The notorious accident that led to his death from reported medical delay, complications, and accusations of incompetence, plus who was really to blame, resounded down the years. Allegedly, the race had been started before all the cars were ready. Another victim of the shambles was Vittorio Brambilla, who suffered serious head injuries and did not race again until the 1979 Italian GP. For Colin Chapman and Lotus it must have seemed like a recurring nightmare, another team driver lost at Monza. This dreadful event even claimed the life of Barbro Peterson, who never got over her loss and committed suicide on 19 December 1987.

⬆ Jean-Pierre Jabouille had been the sole driver of the turbocharged Renault RS01 V6 since its first race at the 1977 British GP. By the end of the 1978 season the car had racked up one DNQ, 13 retirements, one not classified, one 10th place, one 13th place, one 4th place (at Watkins Glen) and one 12th place out of 19 races. At Monza, Jabouille qualified it third-fastest but it only lasted six laps in the restarted race following the accident, before dropping a valve. The Italian GP had descended into a tragic farce as the restarted 40-lap race was won by Mario Andretti with Gilles Villeneuve second, but both were docked one minute for alleged jump starts, perhaps correct for the latter but not the former. So third- and fourth-placed Niki Lauda and John Watson advanced to winner and second place for Brabham, whilst Carlos Reutemann was third for Ferrari.

↗ When March withdrew from F1 Hans Günther Schmidt, of ATS who wanted his own cars to race rather than the Penske PC4 machines used during 1977, bought March's FOCA membership and its F1 interests. The new car was designed by Robin Herd using the PC4 as a base and designated the ATS HS-1 but it was later modified by John Gentry who also penned a 'wing' car, the ATS D1 at the end of 1978. The HS cars were mainly driven by Jean-Pierre Jarier, who departed after the German GP, and Jochen Mass, who left the team after the Dutch race. For Mass it had been a disastrous move after playing second fiddle to Hunt during 1976 and his F1 career never recovered its McLaren status. One of several others who had a go was Keke Rosberg, who drove the aforementioned D1 Gentry wing car and he qualified it 16th out of 26 starters at Watkins Glen but it broke its gear linkage. As ever the ATS is immaculate but the cars were usually hopeless and Schmidt's autocratic management style unacceptable.

➡ After a frustrating year with the new Williams FW06, which had racked up seven retirements and a best placing of fourth (Kyalami), the car came close to winning potential at Watkins Glen. Alan Jones qualified third fastest and finished second behind Reutemann's Ferrari, with the consistent Jody Scheckter third for Wolf. Of the usual suspects, Andretti suffered yet another engine failure, as did both Brabhams, and Hunt finished seventh.

The McLaren M26/5 looks unfamiliar in the gaudy Löwenbrau colours at Montreal, whilst Teddy Meyer's headwear makes him look like a superannuated 12-year-old. Alastair Caldwell is self-evidently thinking something unprintable. This year the Canadian GP was held in Montreal on the Ile de Notre Dame circuit, and by now Hunt had surely lost interest/motivation, qualifying on the penultimate row, and in the race a loose wheel made him run off the track into ankle-deep mud. Both he and Tambay had endured spongy brakes and tyre problems, the Frenchman ending the race in eighth position.

Jean-Pierre Jarier's F1 drives rarely gave him access to a properly competitive car, but in Canada he had the chance and proved his ability beyond any doubt. After the ATS experience, driving the Lotus 79 must have been something of a shock. He raced it first at Watkins Glen, where he qualified eighth but ran out of fuel, and then in Montreal he put it on pole and led the race for 49 laps in the Lotus 79-3. Very sadly an oil-cooler had been holed and the leak caused a terminal drop in oil pressure and also affected the rear brakes. In the other car, Mario Andretti's year had risen to a peak and then crashed down at Monza, and he could only manage tenth here after colliding with Watson's Brabham.

1979

THE LAST FERRARI
CHAMPIONSHIP FOR 21 YEARS

Had the Williams FW06 and later FW07 been more reliable Ferrari would not have won the Constructors' Cup or Jody Scheckter been their World Champion driver. The Didcot team won five grands prix, four courtesy of Alan Jones and Clay Regazzoni one. The points scoring was now being awarded for the four best performances in each half of the year to prevent the championship being decided before the North American races. Scheckter, now ex-Wolf, and Villeneuve won three GPs apiece for Ferrari, the latter losing the title due to more retirements. Renault at last won a race but Lotus did not, the new type 80 was a relative failure and Mario Andretti found himself reverting to the now outpaced 79 later in the season and finishing behind his new team mate Carlos Reutemann, in the championship. Ligier were early season winners but their form fluctuated thereafter and Depailler, who had left Tyrrell, was badly injured in a hang-gliding accident following Monaco and missed the rest of the season. James Hunt had joined the Wolf team but he was unhappy with the car, unmotivated and just walked away from racing after Monaco whilst his McLaren replacement John Watson and Patrick Tambay struggled with the M28 and lamentable M29s. Arrows after their promising 1978 debut faded badly and Tyrrell started off well with a new ground effects car, but could not sustain the effort. As ever there were many grid fillers but possibly the most surprising event of 1979 was that of a disillusioned Niki Lauda leaving Brabham during practice for the Canadian GP (again). The team had endured a mediocre season with the Alfa-engined cars but the late appearance of a DFV-powered BT49 certainly suited Nelson Piquet. On a positive note there were no fatalities in GP racing in the final year of the decade.

Tony Southgate's radical Arrows A2 had first appeared at Dijon and was soon known as the Heinkel bomber on account of its rounded snout and German driver. Its design philosophy and specification are too complex to explain here, but basically its angled engine and gearbox raised the centre of gravity, which caused excessive roll. This also created a problem with change of direction, and it was too heavy. Jochen Mass did his best and squeezed a brace of sixth places out of it, one here at Zandvoort, but it was seriously flawed and another technological dead end.

The New Year began as usual in Argentina with many significant changes amongst the F1 teams. One of these was the final disappearance of Matra's screaming V12s, and the new Gérard Ducarouge-designed Ligier JS11 was just one more Cosworth DFV-powered F1 car. Or perhaps not, as we shall find out. Jacques Lafitte was on pole at the Buenos Aires No. 15 circuit, with his new teammate Patrick Depailler alongside. Behind them were Reutemann, who had gone to Lotus, and Jarier in the new ground effect Tyrrell 009 – so three Frenchmen on the first two rows. The race was halted after the first lap when Scheckter, now Ferrari-mounted, hit Watson, now McLaren-mounted, which triggered an accident that eliminated Jody, Pironi, Tambay, Piquet, and Merzario. At the restart Depailler led for ten laps, after which Lafitte took over, going on to win the race with ease, whilst Depailler dropped back to fourth with uncertain handling and fuel vaporisation issues. This is Carlos Reutemann, in the Lotus 79-2 looking rather drab in the new Martini colour scheme (John Player had ended their motor sport activities), who finished a worthy second at his home GP.

At Interlagos Ligier dominated the front row. This time there were no hiccups and they finished 1/2. Here, Lafitte is welcomed by his joyous team after his second consecutive GP win. Tony Southgate, in his autobiography *From Drawing Board to Chequered Flag*, mentions how designers had to specify very stiff springs to counter excessive downforce at high speed, otherwise the cars would be sucked down to the ground, effectively stalling the 'underwing'. This allowed the car to rise again, thus creating the phenomenon of 'porpoising'. These hard springs caused traction problems at slower corners, something that did not afflict the Ligier. Years later, Tony saw a picture in *Motor Sport* with the Ligier's side panel removed and there was a hidden, very large, spring-loaded hinged panel. This was designed to open at a certain negative pressure, thereby bleeding off excess downforce at high speeds that allowed the Ligier to use softer spring rates. In Southgate's words, 'It was 100% illegal because it was a moveable aerodynamic device which was not allowed.'

J. LAFFITE

ITANES

26

LOCTITE

CHAMPION

KONI

FACOM

⬆ Gordon Murray and David North built a second-generation 'ground effect' car for 1979 with a full length 'underwing', but the Brabham BT48 was afflicted by a constantly moving centre of pressure, which unbalanced the car. Hasty modifications were made in the first race, but it had been designed without use of a wind tunnel and would never be wholly satisfactory, although Piquet would achieve some respectable speed out of it later on. A problem with the wing car configuration was that it was compromised by the architecture of a flat-12, so the BT48 had an Autodelta-built V12 motor. Niki Lauda, seen here in the BT48-2, and Nelson Piquet both retired on lap six of the Brazilian GP, the former with a broken gear linkage, the latter because of a shunt.

↗ At the South African GP the Theodore-sponsored Ensign N179/MN09 featured a large radiator mounted in front of the cockpit, but this was subsequently abandoned, and at Long Beach the car was back to its orthodox side-radiator form. Ironically, despite its macho cooling system, the car was generally overheating and there were other problems too, so Derek Daly failed to qualify at Kyalami. As for the race, the Ligiers had not shone here and both crashed out, whilst Renault had arrived with René Arnoux to complement Jabouille, who posted fastest qualifying time, but both retired. Instead it was Ferrari's new T4 that ruled the roost, with Villeneuve beating Jody Scheckter by under 4sec, and Jarier's Tyrrell a splendid third, beating Andretti's Lotus, which had fading brakes.

➡ Things were improving chez Renault, at least speedwise, but mechanical frailty was still an issue. Jean-Pierre Jabouille placed the Michelin-shod Renault RS 01-02 on pole position here in Kyalami, and when the race was abandoned the first time because of a sudden downpour after two laps he was third, having led the first lap. At the restart Jean-Pierre was in the top four for many laps, but ultimately he retired with a suspected broken valve spring, whilst teammate Arnoux's race ended with a burst tyre after running over debris. Behind the Renault is Scheckter's No. 11 Ferrari, but it is occupied by Villeneuve.

↑ The first start of the US GP (West) at Long Beach was abandoned after Lafitte's Ligier broke its gearbox on the grid. The second start (these had become very fashionable of late) shows the two Ferraris of Villeneuve (No. 12 312T4) and Scheckter leading Depailler's Ligier JS11-03, Andretti's Lotus 79-5, with James Hunt in the Wolf WR8-1 on the outside, and the rest following – like trying to pour a quart into a pint pot.

→ This was the inevitable result, a number of very wide cars approaching at very high speed to find an ever shorter space as the front runners brake to a crawl to get round the hairpin. Patrick Tambay's McLaren M28/3 had gone off line in an attempt to find some room and had slid on the marbles under braking and ridden up the back of Lauda's Brabham BT48/2. Alongside is Jan Lammers in the Samson Shadow DN9/2B that has lost its rear wing in the fracas. Fortunately nobody was hurt this time, and only Lauda and Tambay retired, but 33 years on, circuits are still persisting with chicanes/slow corners after the start, with the same consequences.

↑ A final shot of James Hunt in the twilight of his often-controversial career. Hunt's decision to retire had already been taken in his head, plus he was very unhappy with the car and the way the team was operating. Allowing for any bias in his judgement, James was still apparently capable of hanging out the tail, as evidenced here at Jarama, probably during practice in the Wolf WR8-1. He qualified 16th and retired with braking problems. In Belgium, Hunt briefly ran fourth before crashing, but at Monaco the Wolf retired with a broken CV joint, and so did Hunt, who walked away from the team having lost all interest and possibly his nerve too. At the end of the year a disenchanted Walter Wolf merged his team with the Fittipaldis, and that was the end after just three seasons. The Spanish GP was another Ligier triumph, this time for Depailler, whilst Lafitte retired and Reutemann finished second ahead of Andretti in the new Lotus 80.

↗ Whilst Ferrari and Scheckter celebrated the third Ferrari victory of the year at Zolder, down in the boondocks former F3 star Gianfranco Brancatelli was trying to qualify the Kauhsen WK. The car was the idea of sports car racer Willy Kauhsen and conceived by a Ford Cologne engineer and three professors. The aluminium monocoque was designed by ex-Porsche engineer Kurt Chabek based upon the Lotus 78. The operation was shambolic, the car untried, and Brancatelli, who thankfully later found success in touring cars, failed to make the cut here and in the preceding Spanish GP. Following this, Herr Kauhsen, on the right with clipboard, who had been a successful Porsche racer and principal of his sports car championship-winning Alfa Romeo team in 1975, abandoned any more F1 aspirations.

→ A rather more serious project appeared at Zolder, the long-awaited Alfa Romeo 177 Totale, which was driven by Bruno Giacomelli. It was using the flat-12 motor that was more powerful than Brabham's Autodelta V12, but this was now effectively an outdated design. Nevertheless, Bruno qualified mid-field and raced well enough until he was used as a braking aid by Elio de Angelis's Shadow. Note the police Renault at back of shot as Jack O'Malley passes by – another unadorned car that allows one to see its shape properly.

◄ The Maurice Philippe-designed Tyrrell 009 was an improved version of the Lotus 79, but Ken Tyrrell had lost all his major sponsors. With them had gone the services of ex-Goodyear scientist Dr Karl Kempf, who designed an electronic monitoring system that recorded exactly what was going on in the car at speed, and in turn generated an 'active' ride suspension system which proved very promising, but Tyrrell could no longer afford it. Nevertheless, the 009 and Jarier were doing well, finishing third at Kyalami, sixth at Long Beach, fifth at Jarama, but retiring here at Monaco. More good news was that the Candy sponsorship now gracing the car was reportedly worth $3 million. The Frenchman is chasing Mario Andretti in the Lotus 80, a supposed improvement over the 79, but its gestation was proving difficult and Andretti would retire with a broken rear suspension.

⬆ Glimpsed through the foliage, which is where it should have been, was McLaren's oversize M28B, built upon the mistaken principle that a bigger car would give more downforce and therefore more performance. Patrick Tambay failed to qualify the bloated device at Monaco and, in fact, his form was suffering. Teammate John Watson did qualify and finished fourth in the updated M28C, whilst Jody Scheckter scored his second GP win of the year and Ferrari's fourth, but only just, from a determined Clay Regazzoni in the new Williams FW07. Lotus had something to celebrate, however, with Reutemann finishing third in last year's car.

The slightly off-centre calendar was partly because of the cancellation of the Swedish GP (no folding stuff, you understand), and thus there were two French races back to back. It was a return to Dijon-Prenois for the French GP. This is Hans Stuck, whose former F1 employers had been March, Brabham, and Shadow, but now he had joined the 'maybe I'll qualify' club at ATS. In fact he did not start the ATS D2/03 because Günther Schmidt withdrew the car following a contretemps with Goodyear over the supply of tyres.

Mere photographs cannot do justice to the ferocious duel 'twixt Giles Villeneuve in the Ferrari and René Arnoux in the second Renault at Dijon. Instead, here they are, three French-speaking drivers looking somewhat underwhelmed, with race-winner Jean-Pierre Jabouille flanked by Arnoux (third) and Villeneuve (second). The Ferrari driver's overalls are advertising something called SMEG, which is not a noxious substance but an upmarket Italian manufacturer of domestic appliances. Also present in front of Villeneuve, and looking typically combative, is the delightful Jean-Marie Balestre (9 April 1921 – 21 March 2008) who in 1979 was the President of the Commission Sportive Internationale (CSI).

Without Derek Daly, who had driven for them from mid-1978 up to Monaco 1979, Ensign were struggling to survive even more than usual. At Silverstone, sometime Formula Super Renault, F3, and F2 racer Frenchman Patrick Gaillard was driving the N179, now looking normal, and he just squeezed on to the back of the grid, albeit over 5sec off the pole time of Alan Jones. To his credit he finished (13th), but after not qualifying at Zandvoort he was replaced by Marc Surer.

⬆ It was Alan Jones who could and should have provided the first GP victory for the Williams team at Silverstone. He had been on pole by 0.6sec from Jabouille's Renault and 1.23sec quicker than his teammate, but after leading for 38 laps his development Cosworth engine seized when a water pump seal failed, leaving Clay Regazzoni to win the race. En route Jabouille's Renault had valve spring failure again, but Arnoux finished second, whilst Jarier had another productive drive in the Tyrrell to finish third.

↗ After the frustrations of previous years, Geoff Lees had a one-off drive for Tyrrell at the German GP and finished a worthy seventh in a car he had hardly any knowledge of. Alas, this opportunity only presented itself because Jarier was ill, and Lees never competed in championship F1 again. The race was another Williams triumph, and this time both finished, with Alan Jones heading Regazzoni home comfortably ahead of Lafitte's Ligier.

➡ Look at the difference in attitude of the upper wishbones of the Williams and Ferrari as Jones gets the better of Villeneuve at the Hella-Licht chicane to take the lead on the third lap of the Austrian GP. By lap 11 René Arnoux was also past the Ferrari, followed by Jabouille who was waved past into second by Arnoux, but Jean-Pierre was soon out with gearbox failure because of an inoperative clutch. Towards the end of the race, around lap 50, Arnoux pitted from second place, having run low on fuel, and the Renault dropped to sixth, where it stayed. So Alan Jones won his second straight GP and Williams's third, Villeneuve was second, Jacques Lafitte was third again for Ligier, and Scheckter fourth. Now there were 14 points between championship-leader Scheckter and fifth-placed Regazzoni.

⬆ Another championship-winner from European F3, Elio de Angelis was the Interscope Racing Shadow driver for 1979, whilst Jan Lammers drove the other works car sponsored by Samson. The cultured Italian had an unproductive season and he moved to Lotus in 1980. In Austria he retired with engine failure after 34 laps in the Shadow DN9/3B2.

➡ Patrick Depailler was perhaps what is now known as an adrenalin junkie, and he broke both legs and suffered other serious injuries in a hang-gliding accident on 3 June 1979. This ended his Ligier drive, although he did recover to drive again in F1 for Alfa Romeo but died after crashing at Hockenheim on 1 August 1980. His replacement was Jacky Ickx whose F1 form had long since collapsed, but he did finish fifth here at Zandvoort in the Ligier JS11/01, his best result for a long time, and he finally left F1 after the US GP that October.

↑ Monza was once again the scene for settling the World Championship, and Ferrari did it in style by finishing 1/2 with Jody Scheckter leading Giles Villeneuve across the line to win the title. Both drivers had won three GPs apiece and scored three second places, but it was Jody's four third-place finishes that tipped the balance, and he beat Giles by four points, 51 to 47, with Alan Jones (who actually won four GPs) next on 40 points. It might have been different, however, if Renault's practice form had carried over into the race, as the two turbocharged cars were on the front row, significantly quicker than anybody else, and Arnoux led the race for 11 laps before retiring early on lap 13 with electrical failure. Jabouille, in the other car, was in fourth place after a difficult race, and then it dropped a valve with only five laps to go.

↗ Contrast the profiles of the Ferrari and the new ground effect Alfa Romeo 179 with the driver sitting right at the front of the car. Unlike the 177, the new car had a V12 motor and Giacomelli qualified it on row nine. He reached seventh place during the race, but just as he was closing in on Lauda's Brabham-Alfa he spun off at the Ascari chicane after getting his foot stuck under the brake pedal. Alfa Corse had also entered the old 177 for Vittorio Brambilla, who was making his return to F1 one year on from his head injuries received here during the Peterson accident. The now near 42-year-old finished 12th just one lap down, a good effort with an obsolete car after 12 months away.

→ The penultimate GP of the year was at Montreal again, and it was Alan Jones who won the race after another battle with Gilles Villeneuve, who was determined to repeat his 1978 win here, and they finished less than a second apart. The big news, however, was Niki Lauda's departure from Brabham during first practice. Despite a new car and a good deal for 1980 he remarked, 'My heart is not in it any more.' So Nelson Piquet became the team leader and he had the latest and much better Cosworth-powered Brabham BT49 to play with. He qualified the BT49-02 fourth fastest and spent most of the race in third place until a gearbox failure stopped him on lap 61. The other car was driven by Argentinian Ricardo Zunino, who finished seventh, but his Brabham drive would only last until mid-1980 when Hector Rebaque took over.

↑ Although he had retired quite publicly, Mr Hunt was still around F1, and here he is in the pit lane at Watkins Glen with Mario Andretti. Andretti's post-World Championship season had been a relative disaster. Whereas teammate Carlos Reutemann had achieved two second places, two third, one fourth and one fifth, the American had only one third, two fourths and two fifths to boast of. Mario was racing the old 79-5 at the Glen, the type 80 having been abandoned after the French GP, and he retired here with gearbox failure.

→ Marc Surer's motor racing began with karts and Super Vee, then into the German F3 championship, and from there to F2 and touring car racing for BMW. He made his F1 debut at Monza for Team Ensign, but failed to qualify, followed by the same result in Canada. However, he made it on to the grid at Watkins Glen with the Ensign N179/MN09, and he drove around at the back of the field until his engine broke on lap 32. Swiss-born Surer's career was punctuated by two bad accidents at Kyalami, in 1980 and 1982, and was finally ended by another crash, this time in a German rally in 1986. It left him with career-ending injuries and also killed his co-driver.

↓ Keke Rosberg was the last person to race a works Wolf in a GP before the team was merged with Fittipaldi, and here in the pits Keke shares the pit lane with a prototype built to the new F1 regulations for next year. Peter Warr is smiling about something, but given the year he had endured I cannot imagine what. Rosberg qualified mid-grid in the Wolf WR8/9 and collided with Pironi's Tyrrell on lap 20, which ended his race. The Finn accompanied the cars to Fittipaldi, and amazingly his F1 career survived two poor seasons with them, after which he joined Williams and became the World Champion for his new team. Gilles Villeneuve won the wet race at a canter, 50sec clear of Arnoux's Renault, with Pironi third for Tyrrell, and thus ended a decade of F1.

Returning to this era with a slightly different perspective I was struck by how often the same problems arose over and over again.

Number one on the list was safety. In the face of much press and public vituperation circuits such as Spa-Francorchamps and the Nürburgring were removed from the F1 calendar, in 1970 and 1976 respectively. The use of Armco barriers grew exponentially in period but there were problems with construction, maintenance, and siting. Unrepaired existing damage, not bolted up (these last two as per the 1975 Spanish GP), posts inadequately secured, which allowed the rails to fold over and act as a ramp (Zandvoort 1973), or not suitable for F1 cars, which could pass between or under the rails (Monza 1970, Watkins Glen 1973/74, Kyalami testing 1974), and sometimes accompanied by so-called catch fencing, which could roll up under the crashing car and help launch it over the barriers (1975 Austrian GP).

There were numerous comments reported in the motoring press by spectators and informed persons alike who described Armco as killer barriers at the time. During my research I inevitably came across images of accidents that I have not used for obvious reasons, one being Mark Donohue's fatal incident at the Österreichring in 1975. The site of the crash was the fast right-hander at the top of the hill past the start/finish line and pits, then known as the Vöst-Hurgel curve. There was virtually no run-off, just a few yards if that, between the edge of the track and the barrier, which at various points was shielded by rows of the aforementioned catch fencing. Any car going off track here could not avoid striking the barriers a mighty blow. In this instance the March cleared the top rail and hit one of the scaffolding support poles of a large plastic advertising banner, which inflicted the fatal blow.

Another recurring theme was the number of cars that retired over the decade through failure of fuel metering units, or split fuel lines. Then around the middle of the decade tyres became more vulnerable to punctures and these caused many retirements and quite a few accidents. Of course the ever-increasing speeds and ever-decreasing braking distances exacerbated any such problems, themselves a product of rapidly evolving tyre design, and at this point many of the cars were far from structurally sound. Tyre supply itself also became an issue as said development began to favour chosen teams, or in the case of the Tyrrell P34's unique and tiny front wheels, development ceased thus limiting the car's potential.

Then one must consider the contribution of the Cosworth DFV to the viability of F1 in general from the late 1960s to 1979 and beyond. Without Keith Duckworth and Mike Costin's originally Ford Motor Company funded mechanical masterpiece, there would have been far fewer F1 teams. There were no other suitable engine manufacturers who could supply sufficient units for the majority of an F1 grid.

There were 144 grands prix during the 10 years that separated the South African GP at Kyalami on 7 March 1970 and the US GP East at Watkins Glen on 7 October 1979. Cosworth DFV-powered cars won 99 of these (Lotus 35, Tyrrell 21, McLaren 20, Brabham 6, Williams 5, March 3, Wolf 3, Ligier 3, Hesketh 1, Penske 1 and Shadow 1). The rest were comprised of Ferrari's 37 wins, BRM 4, Brabham-Alfa Romeo 2, and one apiece for Ligier-Matra and Renault.

Ferrari did not supply engines to anybody else, whilst Alfa Romeo's flat-12 and V12 were only available to Brabham and then for Alfa's own F1 car at the end of the decade. The earlier Autodelta V8s used by McLaren and March were unreliable and not powerful enough whilst Matra's V12 was tried by Shadow but soon dropped. This left BRM whose quad-cam V12, a development of the original twin-cam unit, was used solely by the Bourne team and in any case had reached its peak by 1971/72 after which a lack of funding prevented any sustainable development although a short stroke motor was built but it made no impact. A new Weslake-designed V12 had made an appearance in both sports (John Wyer Gulf) and F1 applications (Brabham) but was abandoned.

Seven drivers won the World Championship title in the 1970s, Jochen Rindt, Lotus (posthumously 1970), Jackie Stewart, Tyrrell (1971 and 1973), Emerson Fittipaldi, Lotus and McLaren (1972 and 1974), Niki Lauda, Ferrari (1975 and 1977), James Hunt, McLaren (1976), Mario Andretti, Lotus (1978) and Jody Scheckter, Ferrari (1979). There were 29 individual GP winners in 14 different makes.

A major change was the disappearance of Dunlop from F1 at the end of 1970 leaving Goodyear and Firestone to fight for supremacy. Ultimately Firestone departed too leaving Goodyear as sole supplier until 1977 when Michelin joined the grids with their radial tyres for the newly introduced turbocharged Renault RS.

It was also an era populated by the sudden explosion in sponsorship without which F1 would have gradually stagnated and perhaps disappeared altogether. Inevitably the best teams attracted not only the best drivers but also the most generous backing, thus was born the era of racing cars as mobile advertising boards. At the front of the grid all was well as long as the results were forthcoming but further down the pecking order things were quite desperate at times.

So 'pay drivers' proliferated, some far better than their machinery, others not so. For certain teams it was a hand-to-hand existence and in the case of Surtees and March, who were also manufacturers, one that ultimately could not be borne. As the decade progressed even some of the established teams employed a 'pay driver' of promise who would have come from a successful F3 career complete with a large dowry and who typically would not be British, though there were exceptions.

Along with the media driven commercial interests came more and more races and F1 finally started to expand in the 1970s, but it would be years, decades even, before it could truly claim to be a 'World Championship.'

ACKNOWLEDGEMENTS AND BIBLIOGRAPHY

I would like to thank the following for their help and forbearance in producing this book, many of whom have provided similar assistance for the others in this series:

Doug Nye and Paul Vestey (GP Library), Kevin Wood, Kathy Ager, Tim Wright and Steve Carpenter of LAT Photographic Digital Archive, Peter Sachs (The Klemantaski Collection), Nicola Hartley, Neil Whitaker and Michelle Ryder (Sutton-Images), Mark Hughes, Derek Smith, Christine Smith and Richard Parsons of Haynes Publishing, Jackie Oliver, Helga Oates and my long-suffering wife Sarah Joslin Parker.

I consulted the following published works:

Doug Nye *Autocourse History Of The Grand Prix Car 1966–85* (Hazelton Publishing 1986)

Doug Nye *Mclaren: The Grand Prix, Can-Am And Indy Cars* (Hazelton Publishing 1988)

Alan Henry *Brabham: The Grand Prix Cars* (Hazelton Publishing 1985)

Alan Henry *Ferrari: The Grand Prix Cars* (Hazelton Publishing 1984)

Michael Oliver *Lotus 49: The Story Of A Legend* (Veloce Publishing 1999)

Michael Oliver *Lotus 72: Formula One Icon* (Coterie Press 2003)

Mike Lawrence *The Story Of March: Four Guys And A Telephone* (Aston Publications 1989)

Phil Kerr *To Finish First: My Years Inside Formula One, Can-Am & Indy 500* (MRP Publishing 2008)

Tony Southgate *Tony Southgate: From Drawing Board To Chequered Flag* (MRP Publishing 2010)

Steve Small *Grand Prix Who's Who, Third Edition* (Travel Publishing 2000)

Additionally I referred to the excellent *Autosport* race reports by Paddy McNally and Pete Lyons plus other content, ditto *Motor Sport* courtesy of Denis Jenkinson and Andrew Marriot.